A YEAR OF
QUILTING

ACKNOWLEDGEMENTS

Thank you to Sarah Wickett of
Ambleside Quilting, Workshop and Retreats,
based in Kilkhampton in Cornwall, UK,
who beautifully longarm quilted our final quilt.

First published in 2025

Search Press Limited
Wellwood, North Farm Road,
Tunbridge Wells,
Kent, TN2 3DR
United Kingdom

Text and templates copyright
© Debbie Shore and Melissa Nayler, 2025

Photography by Garie Hind
Copyright © Garie Hind, 2025

Book ISBN: 978-1-80092-046-0
ebook ISBN: 978-1-80093-039-1

SUPPLIERS

For details of suppliers, please see Debbie Shore's website:
www.debbieshoresewing.com

Alternatively, visit the Search Press website:
www.searchpress.com

BOOKMARKED

Digital copies of the templates are also available to
download free from the Bookmarked Hub:
www.bookmarkedhub.com
Search for this book by title or by ISBN number; the files
can be found under 'Book Extras'. Membership of the
Bookmarked online community is free.

MEASUREMENTS & CONVERSIONS

The projects in this book have been made using imperial
measurements, and the metric equivalents provided have
been calculated following standard conversion practices.
The metric measurements are often rounded to the
nearest 0.5cm for ease of use except in rare circumstances;
however, if you need more exact measurements, there are
a number of excellent online converters that you can use.
Always use either metric or imperial measurements, not a
combination of both.

FURTHER INSPIRATION

For more information about Debbie Shore, visit:
▸ her website, www.debbieshoresewing.com
▸ her YouTube channel, via @debbieshore
▸ her Instagram page, via @debbieshore
▸ her Facebook page, via @debbieshoresewing
▸ Half Yard™ Sewing Club: www.halfyardsewingclub.com

MIX
Paper | Supporting
responsible forestry
FSC® C136333
FSC
www.fsc.org

A YEAR OF
QUILTING

A BLOCK FOR EVERY WEEK

DEBBIE SHORE & MELISSA NAYLER

SEARCH PRESS

Contents

THE BLOCKS 52

ASSEMBLY, QUILTING & FINISHING 146

INSPIRATIONAL BLOCKS 164

TEMPLATES 168

INTRODUCTION

If you've been thinking about making a large quilt, but found the idea of it overwhelming, this is the book for you!

Similar to the Block a Month concept that's popular in the patchwork and quilting world, we've designed our quilt to be made a block at a time, once a week, over the course of a year. Gradually, over 12 months, you'll create a stunning quilt in achievable bite-size chunks, allowing you to fit your quilting passion in around your busy life.

All the blocks in this book come together to create a 72 x 60in (183 x 152.5cm) quilt. The blocks are numbered by week, but you can make them in any order you wish; you can also make as many blocks as you have time for (it doesn't have to take a year to complete the quilt!).

Some blocks you may find easy to make; others may be slightly more challenging. You'll be able to try out techniques you may not have attempted before, as well as pick up some shortcuts and useful tips along the way. If you're new to quilting and patchwork, we've ordered the blocks so that the first few weeks gently introduce you to different techniques, helping you gain confidence to tackle the slightly more challenging designs that you'll find in later weeks. Alongside the block patterns, we've provided a Key Techniques section that gives comprehensive instructions for making up the blocks.

At the back of our book, you'll find a few inspirational ideas of how to transform some of the blocks into different items such as homewares and accessories.

Some of the blocks require templates, and these are all provided at the back of the book at full-size, with no need to re-scale. Some of the appliqué templates are accompanied by placement diagrams, to help you position them correctly in the final block; please note these diagrams are not to scale, and are to be used as references only.

We hope you have fun making your quilt and, if you'd like to, please share your final piece on either Facebook or Instagram with this hashtag: #ayearofquiltingbyDandM

BEFORE YOU BEGIN

◊ **Fabric abbreviations:** We've used nine different fabrics to create the quilt top – five patterned, three plain/solid and one white-on-white. The exact requirements are detailed on page 9. Throughout the book, the patterned and plain fabrics will be referred to as Fab A–Fab H, and the white-on-white background fabric as WW. As you will likely use different fabrics to us, we recommend making your own swatch key of fabrics, as we've done on page 9, so you have your own visual references to check when you start making a new block. If you're making the quilt using a selection of fabrics from your stash, rather than purchasing them new, just ensure you have a balanced spread of colours across the quilt.

◊ **Block instructions:** For each block, read through the instructions carefully before making a start.

◊ **'Key Techniques':** Keep referring back to this chapter for guidance. Each block details the techniques used to make it up.

◊ **Seam allowance:** Stitch with an accurate ¼in (5mm) seam allowance throughout, unless otherwise stated.

◊ **'Unfinished size of block':** Any reference to this refers to the size before sewing the block into the quilt (i.e. the size of the block with the seam allowance included).

◊ **Right side or wrong side?:** Sew all seams with the right sides (RS) of the fabric facing, unless otherwise stated.

◊ **Pressing seams:** Before pressing seam allowances, run a hot iron along the length of your stitching. This helps the stitches to sink into the fabric, and will make the seam allowances easier to press.

Generally, seam allowances are pressed towards the darker fabric. However, in some cases, to avoid bulk it is necessary to press towards the lighter fabric or to press the seam open – this will be indicated in the individual block instructions. If you prefer to press all your seams open, that's fine.

◊ **Diagonal edges:** Take care stitching shapes that have diagonal edges, as these can stretch. Lightly spraying the shape with starch, before sewing, may help.

◊ **Raw edge appliqué templates**: All of these are provided at the back of the book in reverse, which is necessary if using fabric adhesive sheets. If using spray adhesive or stitching with needleturn appliqué (see page 39), you'll need to flip the templates (so they are the right way round) before preparing them for appliqué.

◊ **Pre-washing your fabric:** Whether you wash your fabric before cutting and sewing is entirely your choice. If you decide to wash but like the look of a more crinkled, 'antique' style of quilt, then wash after its construction, otherwise wash, dry and press all your fabrics before you start (light machine washing is fine). If there's any chance of your fabric 'bleeding', then definitely pre-wash; if you're not sure, check on a sample first. If you do decide to pre-wash you'll be removing some of the sizing, which adds a stiffness to the fabric; so, we would suggest lightly spraying starch on your fabrics after they are washed and dried, to help with accurate cutting and piecing. All fabrics, whether pre-washed or not, should be ironed before you cut them.

◊ **Cut your fabric conservatively:** This is particularly important when cutting out your background fabric, as there are several larger blocks in the quilt and you don't want to run out of fabric before you get to them. Wherever possible, always use up any scraps of fabric as you work your way through the quilt, which will minimize wastage and ensure you get as much as you can out of your fabrics.

REQUIREMENTS

FABRICS

Each fabric's quantities are listed alongside its swatch and abbreviations. Yardage is based on a 44in (112cm) width of fabric. As noted on page 7, we recommend being conservative when cutting out fabric to reduce wastage, and to ensure you have enough to successfully sew all the blocks in the book without running out of fabric.

FAB A
Orange print,
1yd (1m)

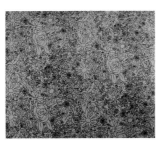

FAB B
Turquoise print,
1yd (1m)

FAB C
Black print,
1yd (1m)

FAB D
Pale blue print,
1yd (1m)

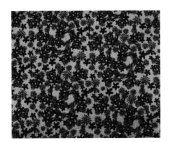

FAB E
Magenta print,
¾yd (0.75m)

FAB F
Purple plain,
¾yd (0.75m)

FAB G
Dark red plain,
1yd (1m)

FAB H
Yellow plain,
1yd (1m)

WW
White-on-White,
3¼yd (3m)

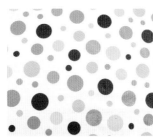

BACKING FABRIC
4½yd (4m)

BINDING FABRIC
(We used Fab D)
¾yd (0.75m)

THREADS

We recommend a selection of matching and contrasting sewing threads. A 50–60wt cotton or polyester thread is suitable for machine piecing. For needleturn appliqué (see page 39), use a similar thread in a colour to match the appliqué piece. For English Paper Piecing (see page 46), use a finer thread that's suitable for bobbins, for example bobbin fill or silk thread. For machine quilting, there's a variety of threads you can use, depending on your preferred finished look. For hand quilting, use a special hand-quilting thread, which is slightly thicker than regular sewing thread.

BATTING/WADDING

You'll need a Twin (UK single) size pack (72 x 90in, or 183 x 228.5cm) of batting/ wadding for this quilt.

Batting/wadding is the padded layer that goes between the quilt top and the quilt's backing. An 80/20 cotton/polyester blend of batting/wadding is ideal for machine and hand quilting. If you need to join pieces of batting/wadding, butt the two edges together (don't overlap them) and stitch together either with a large zigzag stitch on a sewing machine or with herringbone stitch by hand.

OTHER MATERIALS

◊ **Fabric adhesive sheets:** These are used for securing appliqué shapes to a background fabric, before stitching them down. The sheets are placed between the appliqué and background fabrics then ironed to fuse the two layers in place permanently. The paper backing on the adhesive sheet is particularly useful: you can draw your shape on it before cutting it out, creating an accurate design. Once the shape is adhered to the appliqué fabric and cut out, the paper side is then removed before pressing to fuse the shape into position onto the background fabric.

◊ **Paper and lightweight card:** These are for reproducing templates and piecing papers (for example English Paper Piecing and Foundation Paper Piecing; see pages 46–51 for more information about these techniques).

◊ **Freezer paper:** This is optional but useful for certain types of appliqué – see page 41 for more information.

◊ **Interfacing:** This is a lightweight fabric used mainly in dressmaking to give hidden support to facings, cuffs, collars and ties. It's usually purchased by the metre; for this book's quilt, half a metre would be ample. We have used it to add structure to some blocks; if you don't have access to interfacing, you could also use stabilizer or even thin copy paper. Copy paper will need to be removed after stitching.

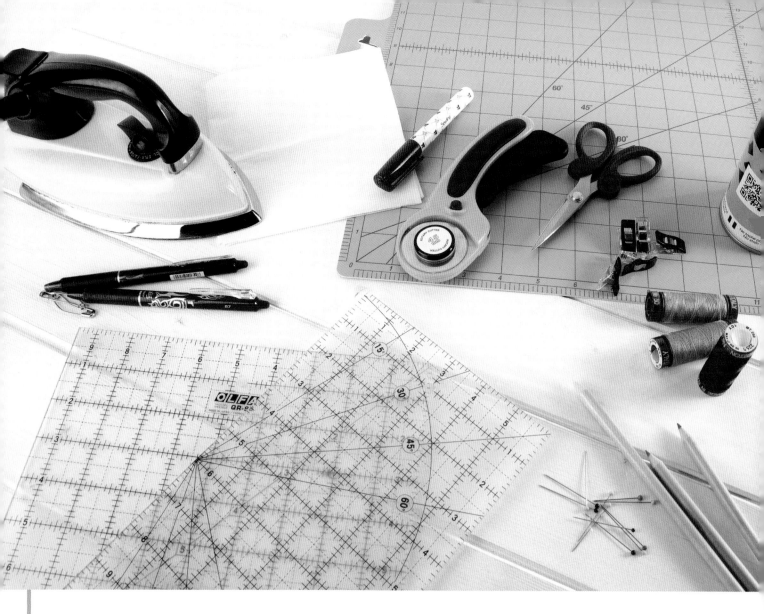

TOOLS

◊ **Sewing machine:** You don't need a fancy machine to stitch a quilt, as really only straight and zigzag stitches are used. However, you will need to be able to move the needle up/down, install a walking (dual-/even-feed) foot, and drop the feed dogs (the little teeth in the needle plate that grip the fabric when sewing).

◊ **Fabric/dressmaking scissors.**

◊ **Iron.**

◊ **Rotary cutter:** This is very useful for patchwork, as it allows you to cut small pieces of fabric quickly and accurately. A 45mm-blade rotary cutter is the most useful size, 28mm cutters are useful for cutting around curves or following acrylic templates, and 60mm blades will make light work of multiple layers of fabric. Always cover the blade with a safety guard after every cut (this will soon become a habit), as rotary cutter blades are incredibly sharp. Always dispose of the blades safely – even a blade that you'd consider to be blunt can still be dangerous. Many rotary cutters can be adjusted for left- or right-handed cutting.

◊ **Cutting mat:** If you will be using a rotary cutter, you'll need a mat to protect both your table and the blade of your rotary cutter – the larger the better! Some mats will have inches on one side and centimetres on the other, with many diagonal markings for bias cutting and measuring angles. Try to store your mat flat when not in use to prevent it buckling, and keep it clean. A self-healing cutting mat is a worthwhile investment – the cuts you make simply close over, prolonging the life of your mat.

◊ **Quilting ruler:** We recommend a 24 x 6in (61 x 15cm) ruler with ⅛in (3mm) increments. You'll find 30-degree, 45-degree and 60-degree markings, and these are useful for measuring on the bias or marking grids on your fabric for quilting. Some rulers are frosted so that the grid lines stand out against your fabric; some have markings in black and white for the same reason. The ruler you use with a rotary cutter should be at least ⅛in (3mm) thick to prevent the blade from slipping over the ruler when cutting.

◊ **Square ruler with 45-degree angle line:** This is optional but useful. There are smaller sizes available on the market, but if you decide to invest in one it's best to get the largest you can find – such as a 12in (30.5cm) or a 16in (40.5cm) size – as all the smaller sizes are included.

◊ **Pins and quilting clips:** We like to use glass-headed pins for a couple of reasons – they can be seen if they're dropped, and won't melt if you accidentally iron them! Fabric clips are a great alternative to pins when working with lots of layers or if you have dexterity issues.

◊ **Hand-stitching needles:** Needles vary in length, point shape and thickness depending on their purpose. We suggest keeping a pack of Sharps in various sizes in your sewing kit for general use. Needles designed especially for hand quilting are called 'Betweens'; these are small, strong needles with a round eye. Their size and strength mean they can pass through multiple layers yet still create small stitches.

◊ **Seam ripper/quick unpick:** We all make mistakes! It's also useful for removing basting/tacking stitches.

◊ **Erasable fabric marker:** Whether you're free-hand drawing or using templates and rulers, you will probably have to mark your fabric at some point. There are lots of products on the market to choose from! Often we use either air-erasable, water-erasable or heat-erasable pens, and each one has its advantages and disadvantages. We recommend testing one of each type yourself, so you pick the pen that's right for your way of working.

◊ **Fabric spray adhesive:** For a quick alternative to basting/tacking, you can spray your fabric with this instead. It's very useful for holding layers of fabric and batting/wadding together when assembling and quilting them together.

◊ **Fabric glue pen:** This is very useful for securing fiddly sections of your work, such as securing the seam allowance to the paper template in English Paper Piecing (see page 46).

◊ **Spray starch:** This is optional but is useful for making the fabric easier to finger-press and to stabilize bias edges.

◊ **Thin paint brush:** Optional tool, we use this sometimes to apply starch to seam allowances.

TEMPLATES

Full-size templates will be provided where necessary. You will need to reproduce these by photocopying, tracing or using your preferred method. To reproduce placement templates for appliqué, a lightbox is useful but not essential. If you don't have a light box, attach the template to a window or glass door with the fabric placed on top and mark accordingly.

KEY TECHNIQUES

This section of the book serves as a reference guide while creating your quilt; plus, you can revisit it as a learning tool and reminder for any future makes.

Various patchwork techniques are used to make the *A Year of Quilting* quilt. If you're a confident beginner, follow them to increase your patchwork skills; for those more experienced, experiment and expand on the basic techniques to create individual designs that will make your quilt unique.

If you're reasonably new to patchwork and quilting, you may wish to try out the techniques on scrap fabric before you start. The samples explored in each method on the following pages are a snapshot of each technique and do not necessarily replicate the final blocks in the quilt, the fabrics in particular.

If you don't want to make a full-size quilt, take a look at the inspirational makes at the back of the book, then have a go at re-interpreting your own blocks to make accessories and more.

HAND STITCHES

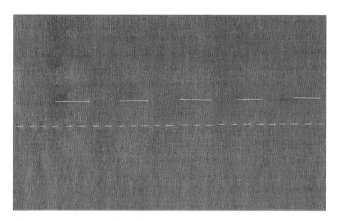

Running stitch

Use this as a basting/tacking stitch, or to gather fabric when the thread is pulled (see top line). If they are made tiny, the stitches can be as strong as machine stitches (see bottom line).

Whip/overcast stitch

This is used for sewing two pieces of fabric together, particularly in English Paper Piecing (see page 46). Take the needle through the fabric, over the edge and back through again a little way along.

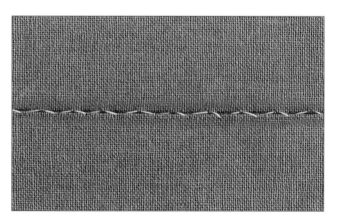

Slip stitch

We use this for hand appliqué. Bring a threaded needle up through the fold of the seam allowance around the appliqué piece, catching just a few threads, then take the needle back down into the background fabric. Repeat all around. Keep the stitch to a short length and try to just catch a couple of strands of the fold of the fabric to keep the stitch as invisible as possible.

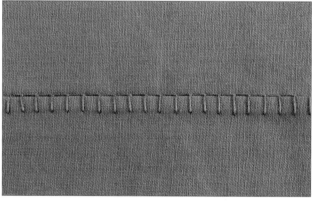

Blanket stitch

This stitch gives a lovely hand-made look when appliquéing, and really stands out when embroidery thread is used. Bring a threaded needle up about ¼in (5mm) from the edge of the fabric. Take it over the edge then back down into the fabric, close to your starting point. Before drawing the thread completely, take the needle through the loop you made. Repeat all along the edge of your piece.

MACHINE STITCHES

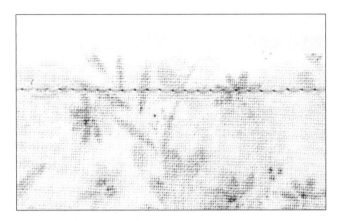

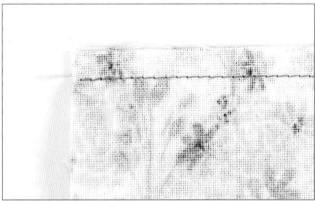

Straight stitch

The most useful stitch on your machine! Straight stitch is used for joining fabric, top-stitching, and – if you alter the length – gathering and basting/tacking.

Back-tacking/reverse stitch

Whenever starting and ending a length of stitches, reverse a couple of stitches to stop the row coming undone. Some sewing machines have a locking stitch, which puts a few stitches in the same place to secure before sewing, meaning you don't need to reverse manually.

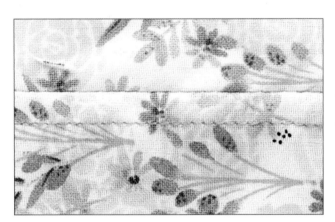

Top-stitch & edge-stitch

Top-stitch is a straight stitch that is deliberately made visible on the front of your project, and is usually worked ¼in (5mm) from the edge of a seam. Edge-stitch is almost the same as top-stitch, but is worked much closer to the seam – usually ⅛in (3mm).

Zigzag & satin stitch

Typically used along hems or raw edges to stop fabric from fraying, zigzag stitch has been used in our quilt to add a decorative edge around some of the appliqué shapes. The width of zigzag stitch can be altered on your sewing machine to accommodate your project. If the width is narrowed it creates a satin-stitch effect.

CHAIN PIECING

Also known as continuous stitching, chain piecing is a useful technique when you wish to sew together multiple pairs of fabric pieces (often units within a block) very quickly. Pairs are sewn one after the other in a long chain, without cutting the thread in between – you just continue to run a few stitches between each unit (don't worry, it won't harm your machine) – see **Fig. A**. This method will not only save you time but thread too.

If you're struggling with your fabric disappearing into your sewing machine's feed dogs, start your stitching by sewing across a narrow folded scrap of fabric, followed by a few stitches off the fabric (**Fig. B**), then start your specific sewing. When you've finished stitching, place another scrap of folded fabric under your needle before cutting your threads (**Fig. C**); the scrap is then ready to start your next piece of sewing (**Fig. D**). Not only will this trick stop your machine 'eating' your fabric, it's a great time-saver if your machine does not have a thread cutter.

After you've finished chain piecing all the necessary pairs of fabric pieces, cut the threads in between your chain pieced units.

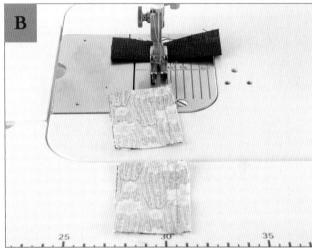

MACHINE PIECING

Machine piecing is very popular with both traditional and contemporary patchworkers and is used to make up blocks to create many of the quilts we see today. For precision, fabric is usually cut to size using a rotary cutter, ruler and a self-healing mat, then machine pieced together with an accurate ¼in (5mm) seam allowance to form the block. Accuracy of the seam allowance is key, and as long as it is consistent throughout the project your patchwork blocks will match up.

On pages 19–36 we'll explore all the machine piecing techniques used for the quilt.

A couple of tips to bear in mind:

◊ First, for all the **techniques that involve stitching across the diagonal** then folding back the piece and cutting off the excess fabric, stitch a thread's width extra on the side of the diagonal you'll be pressing towards. This will ensure your corner piece does not come up short.

◊ Second, **before cutting off the excess seam allowance**, press your seam line and fabric back; this will give you an indication of exactly where your fabric should sit when pressed.

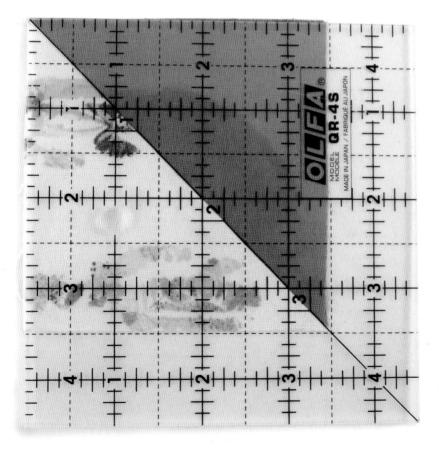

Trimming a block with a square ruler. Note the 45-degree line matches the diagonal seam.

Square Triangles

The use of Half Square, Quarter Square and Split Quarter Square triangles in quilts has become very popular and there are various ways of making one at a time or in multiples. We tend to make ours slightly larger than required and then trim to size for accuracy. Where these units are used in this book, appropriate cutting instructions are provided.

TIP

Many of the blocks in the quilt will have sets of triangles cut off. Some will be too small for re-use, but others could be stitched together along the diagonal seam line to create a smaller Half Square Triangle. Store them in your stash for use at a later date.

SINGLE HALF SQUARE TRIANGLE

I. Cut two squares of contrasting fabric that are the unfinished size of the desired Half Square Triangle unit.

2. On the wrong side (WS) of one square (usually the lighter fabric), draw a diagonal line from one top corner to the opposite bottom corner with a pencil or fabric marker (it doesn't matter which way).

3. With right sides (RS) together, stitch along the line.

4. Trim one side of the seam to a ¼in (5mm) seam allowance.

5. Either press the seam open or, if you prefer, press towards the darker fabric. Store the leftover triangles in your stash for a future project.

TWO-IN-ONE HALF SQUARE TRIANGLES

I. Cut two squares of contrasting fabric that are 1in (2.5cm) larger than the finished size of your desired Half Square Triangle unit. On the wrong side (WS) of one square (usually the lighter fabric), draw a diagonal line from top to bottom with a pencil or fabric marker (it doesn't matter which way).

2. With right sides (RS) together, sew a ¼in (5mm) away from each side of the drawn line, then cut in half along the line (**Fig. A**).

3. Either press the seams open or, if you prefer, press towards the darker fabric.

4. Using your square ruler, line up the 45-degree angle along the seam line of one square then trim the square to the required unfinished size. Make sure you cut off the 'ears' at the corners of your unit. Trim the second square in the same way. Your two units are complete (**Fig. B**).

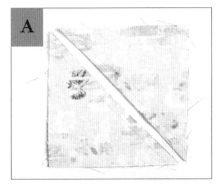

A

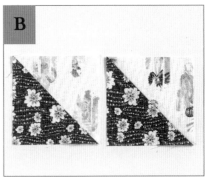

B

FOUR-IN-ONE
HALF SQUARE TRIANGLES

With the following method, the outside edges will be on the bias. A light spray of starch will help to stabilize them when stitching them into the quilt later.

I. Cut two contrasting squares of fabric to the same size. To calculate the size of the two squares, divide the unfinished size of the Half Square Triangle unit (i.e. the size before it's sewn into the quilt) by 0.64 and round the figure up to the nearest ¼in (5mm).

2. With right sides (RS) together, start by sewing a ¼in (5mm) seam allowance all the way around the outer edge. Cut two diagonal lines across the square, from corner to corner, to create four Half Square Triangles, being careful not to move the pieces during cutting (**Fig. A**).

3. Either press the seams open or, if you prefer, press towards the darker fabric.

4. Using your square ruler, line up the 45-degree angle along the seam line on one square then trim the square to the required unfinished size. Make sure you cut off the 'ears' on the corners of your unit. Trim the remaining squares in the same way (**Fig. B**).

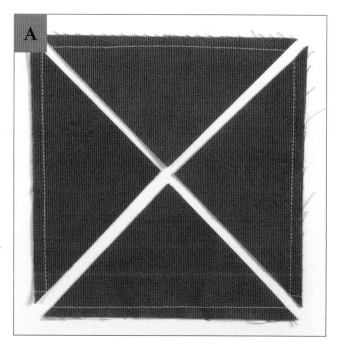

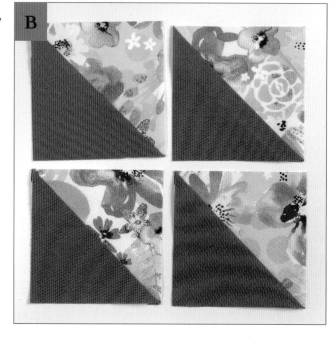

Technique used for Week 23: Star 5.
See page 90.

EIGHT-IN-ONE
HALF SQUARE TRIANGLES

1. Cut two contrasting squares of fabric to the same size. To calculate the size of the two squares, add 1in (2.5cm) to the desired finished Half Square Triangle size, then multiply by 2. (If you want to make your squares slightly larger to accommodate more generous trimming, add another ¼in or 5mm to the size of both squares.)

2. Mark both the diagonal lines on the wrong side (WS) of one square. Pin the two squares right sides (RS) together and stitch ¼in (5mm) away from each side of both diagonals (**Fig. A**).

3. Cut the squares in half through the middle, from top to bottom, then from one side to the other. Then cut along all the drawn diagonal lines. You should now have eight cut pieces (**Fig. B**).

4. Press the seams towards the darker fabric. Using your square ruler, line up the 45-degree angle along the seam line of one square then trim the square to the required unfinished size. Make sure you cut off the 'ears' on the corners of your unit (**Fig. C**). Trim the remaining squares in the same way.

Technique used for Week 35: Large Pieced Block 2. See page 110.

SPLIT HALF SQUARE TRIANGLES

1. Make a Single Half Square Triangle unit, following the cutting and making-up instructions on page 19 (**Fig. A**).

2. Cut a square from a third contrasting fabric measuring the size of your unfinished unit/Single Half Square Triangle. Draw a diagonal line on the wrong side (WS) of the third square fabric. Place the square on top of the pieced unit, right sides (RS) together and ensuring the diagonal line is perpendicular to the previously stitched seam (**Fig. B**).

3. Stitch along the line then trim the left-hand side to a ¼in (5mm) seam allowance.

4. Either press the seam open or, if you prefer, press towards the darker fabric (**Fig. C**). Store the left-over triangles in your stash for a future project.

Technique used for Week 42: Star 8.
See page 122.

QUARTER SQUARE TRIANGLES

The following instructions will produce two identical units.

1. Add 1½in (4cm) to the desired finished size of your Quarter Square Triangle unit then make two Half Square Triangle units, following the instructions for the Two-in-One Half Square Triangles on page 19 (**Fig. A**).

2. On the wrong side (WS) of one Half Square Triangle, draw a diagonal line running in the opposite direction to the seam line. Position this unit on top of the second Half Square Triangle, right sides (RS) together and with contrasting fabrics facing (**Fig. B**). The drawn diagonal line (see the black line) should be perpendicular to the stitched seam on the bottom unit, but the seams should of both units should match – the purple dashed line is the seam for the bottom unit, and the red dashed line is the seam of the top unit.

3. Stitch ¼in (5mm) away from each side of the drawn line, then cut along the drawn line. Either press the seam open or, if you prefer, press towards the darker fabric.

4. Using your square ruler, line up the 45-degree angle along the seam line of one square then trim the square to the required unfinished size. Make sure you cut off the 'ears' on the corners of your unit. Trim the remaining squares in the same way (**Fig. C**).

Technique used for Week 31: Star 6.
See page 106.

Half Rectangle Triangles

These units differ to Half Square Triangles because they are directional: the direction you sew your diagonal makes a difference to the finished appearance.

With this method you will be creating two identical Half Rectangle Triangles, which will be trimmed with the aid of a template. We like to use freezer paper, but stabilizer or photocopy paper can be used. If you're using freezer paper, you will need to draw on the non-shiny side, as the shiny side will be temporarily adhered to the fabric.

1. Let's start by creating a template. On a sheet of paper, draw a rectangle measuring the desired finished size (i.e. after the unit has been sewn into the quilt) then mark an 'X' from corner to corner. Cut out the rectangle (**Fig. A**).

2. To work out how big to cut your fabric, divide the longest edge (length) of the desired finished rectangle by its shortest edge (width) to establish the ratio. For any size rectangle, always add 1½in (4cm) to the width; with the length, add 1½in (4cm) if the ratio is 1:1.5, or 2in (5cm) if the ratio is greater.

3. Cut out your two contrasting fabrics to the measurements calculated in the previous step. On the wrong side (WS) of one rectangle, draw a diagonal line in the opposite direction to where you want the diagonal to be on the finished block. Place the rectangle on top of the other, right sides (RS) together. Before you stitch, rotate the top rectangle by a quarter turn then realign the corners – we rotated ours counter-clockwise (see the purple arrow in **Fig. B**). Stitch ¼in (5mm) along each side of the drawn diagonal line (see the dashed purple lines in **Fig. B**).

4. Cut along the drawn line then press the seams open. You will have two identical Half Rectangle Triangles (**Fig. C**).

5. Position the template from Step 1 on the RS of one Half Rectangle Triangle, matching the diagonal line on both the stitched unit and the template. Allow for at least a ¼in (5mm) seam allowance all around the outside of the template (**Fig. D**). If you're using freezer paper, press into position (shiny side down) with an iron to hold in place, otherwise pin. Cut out the shape, adding ¼in (5mm) seam allowance (**Fig. E**). Remove the template (**Fig. F**). Repeat Step 5 with the remaining Half Rectangle Triangle.

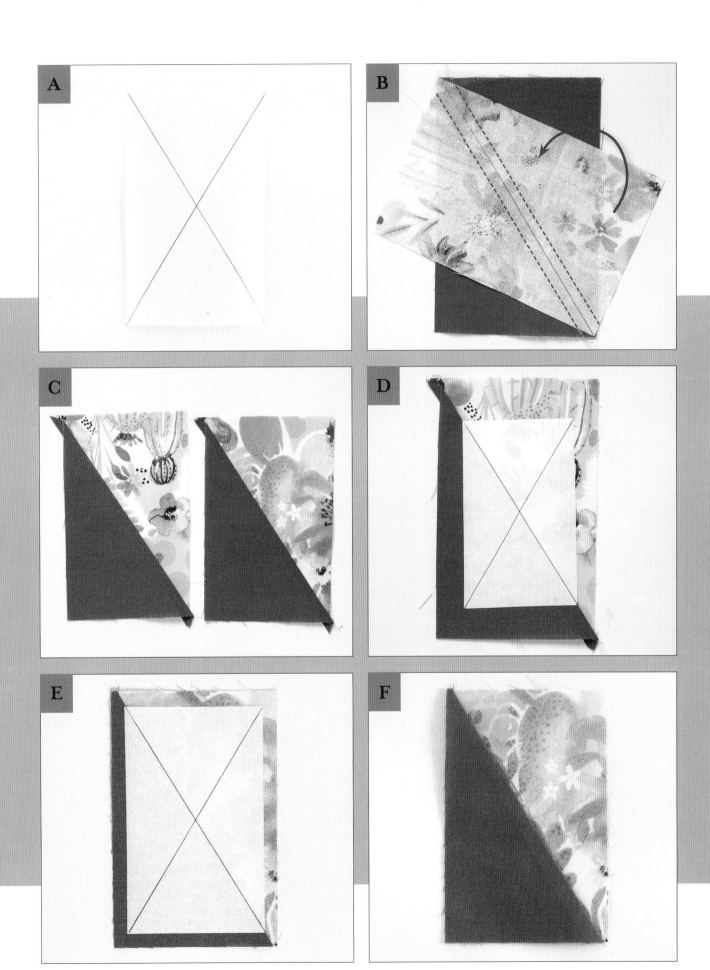

Flying Geese

These units have always been a popular addition to any quilt, either within the main quilt design or as part of a border, and are quick and easy to produce. For a border design, these can be made up in multiples. Several variations of Flying Geese are included in the quilt in this book. Below and opposite are techniques for the two most common versions; specific details for other versions are included in the instructions for the individual blocks.

SINGLE FLYING GEESE

For each individual Flying Geese unit one rectangle and two contrasting squares will be required (exact cutting details will be given in the block instructions).

I. On the wrong side (WS) of each square, draw a diagonal line from one corner to the other – it's essential this line is drawn accurately into the corners (**Fig. A**).

2. With right sides (RS) together, position the first square on top of the rectangle, matching the side edges and with the diagonal going from top inside to bottom outer. Stitch along the drawn line then trim the top edge to a ¼in (5mm) seam allowance (see the pink line in **Fig. B**) and press upwards. Repeat on opposite side of the rectangle (see the blue line in **Fig. B**).

3. **Fig. C** shows the finished unit.

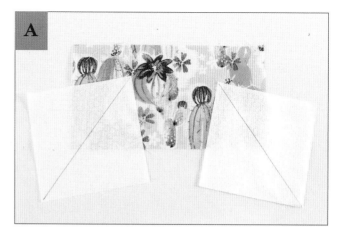

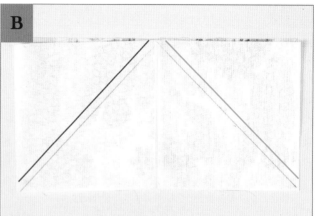

Technique used for Week 6: Bird 1.
See page 61.

FOUR-IN-ONE FLYING GEESE

This method creates four identical Flying Geese units at the same time. Precise sizes will be given in the quilt instructions.

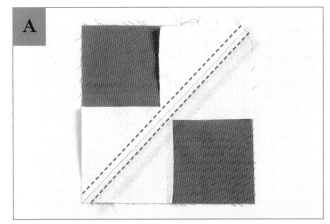

1. Cut one large square and four smaller squares – we've used orange fabric for the large square, and white fabric for the smaller squares. With right sides (RS) together, position two of the smaller squares over the larger square at opposite corners – they will slightly overlap each other in the middle. Draw a diagonal line from corner to corner across both smaller squares, then stitch ¼in (5mm) away from each side of the line (see the purple dashed lines in **Fig. A**).

2. Cut along the marked line to create two units. Then, for each unit, press the two smaller triangles away from the larger triangle (**Fig. B**).

3. Take one of the units. With RS together, position a third small square on the lower corner of the large triangle. Again, draw a line corner to corner on the smaller square. Sew either side of the line as before (see the purple dashed lines in **Fig. C**) – see also the tip below. Cut along the marked line. Press the smaller triangles away from the larger triangle to complete the first two Flying Geese units.

TIP: Stitch these final two seams in the same direction, starting in the centre and working towards the outer corner – this ensures that both sides of the Flying Geese meet neatly at the centre top.

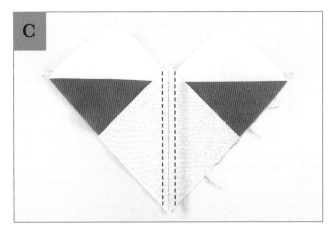

4. Repeat Steps 3 and 4 with the remaining unit and the fourth small square to create four Flying Geese units in total (**Fig. D**). If you need to trim, position the square ruler over half the unit so the edge matches the centre point and the 45-degree angle line matches the diagonal seam. Trim. Turn the unit around and trim the other side in the same way.

Crazy Patchwork

This is a fun piecing technique that involves joining together various shapes in different fabrics to create a random, unique design. It's a great way to use up fabric scraps. (If your scraps are too small to begin with, just join two or three together to create a larger piece before adding them to your crazy patchwork.)

It's usual to start in the centre (or slightly off-centre) and create a shape with no particular number of sides – just add contrasting fabric strips and shapes, working around the centre outwards to create a unique piece of fabric (**Fig. A**). Once you've achieved the desired size (plus 1–2in/2.5–5cm extra, to accommodate any unusual angles), just trim the edges square. If you prefer, draw up a Foundation Paper Piecing-like grid to use as a guide (see page 49 for more on Foundation Paper Piecing) and stitch your Crazy Patchwork using that technique.

For a striking quilt top, join several Crazy Patchwork blocks together with strips of sashing in the same colourway to create some cohesion. Traditional Crazy Patchwork is often embellished with hand or machine embroidery stitched over seam lines, with lace, ribbon, ric rac and beads added to create even more interest (**Fig. B**).

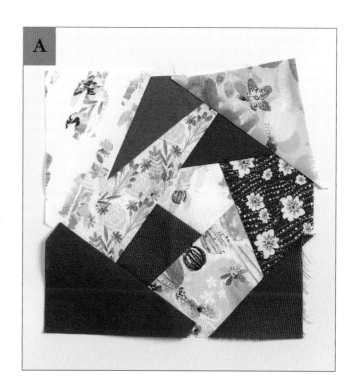

Checkerboard

Several blocks in this quilt feature a checkerboard pattern, and this block design is one of the most popular (and easiest) to make. The two most common checkerboard designs are the Four Patch and Nine Patch.

FOUR PATCH

Cut four squares, two in one colourway and two in another. Stitch contrasting squares right sides (RS) together in pairs, then stitch the two pairs RS together with contrasting fabrics facing to create your four-patch checkerboard (**Fig. A**).

NINE PATCH

1. Cut three squares of fabric, one in the main fabric and two in the contrasting fabric. Stitch the squares right sides (RS) together, ensuring the main fabric is in the middle (**Fig. B**).

2. Cut three strips of fabric – two in the main fabric and one in the contrast fabric – that measure the height of the original squares but twice the width. With the contrast fabric in the middle, stitch these strips RS together along the long edges. Cut the joined strips in half, across the seams, into two equal-sized strips (**Fig. C**); once rotated by 90 degrees, they should be the same length as the unit in Step 1.

3. To complete the unit, with RS together stitch one strip from Step 2 above the row made in Step 1, then stitch the remaining strip to the bottom of the row made in Step 1 (**Fig. D**).

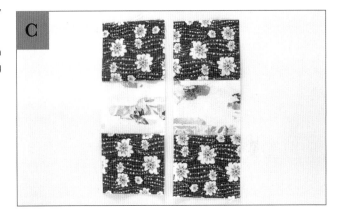

Log Cabin

This is a popular, traditional block that typically uses contrasting strips of light and dark fabrics to create a design that spirals from the inside outwards. It doesn't matter if your block spirals in a clockwise or counter-clockwise direction; however, once you've established the direction, it's essential that every new piece added continues in that direction (e.g. if all the pieces in the first 'circuit' were added clockwise, the rest of the 'circuits' must have their pieces added in a clockwise direction too).

Accurate cutting and stitching is required to ensure the block remains square as you work around the initial inner square piece of fabric (which is traditionally red in colour, to represent the hearth of the home). To help with accuracy, we like to starch our fabrics before cutting them, and if necessary measure and trim the block square each time a 'circuit' of the block is completed.

There are several different Log Cabin designs; opposite is the traditional Log Cabin design that spirals outwards from the centre, and is the one used in our quilt.

I. Start by cutting all your strips the same width – in the example here, the strips are 1½in (4cm) wide. Cut then stitch a 1½in (4cm) square of centre fabric (ours is red) and 1½in (4cm) square of dark fabric right sides (RS) together and press (**Fig. A**).

2. Rotate your block in your chosen direction. Cut a second strip of dark fabric measuring 2½in (6.5cm) long, then stitch this to one side of your joined shape (**Fig. B**). First 'circuit' complete. Square up your block if necessary.

3. Rotate the block in the same direction as before. Cut then add your first light strip, measuring 2½in (6.5cm) in length (**Fig. C**).

4. Repeat Step 3 to add another light strip, this time measuring 3½in (9cm) in length (**Fig. D**).

5. Continue as above, always rotating in the same direction, to add six more strips in the following lengths and colours: dark, 3½in (9cm) in length; dark, 4½in (11.5cm) in length (second 'circuit' complete, square up your block if necessary); light, 4½in (11.5cm) in length; light, 5½in (14cm) in length; dark, 5½in (14cm) in length; dark, 6½in (16.5cm). Square up your block if necessary (**Fig. E**).

Dresden Plate

This is another traditional block that has seen a resurgence in recent years. Popular in the 1920s and 1930s, the Dresden Plate features a selection of different fabrics (often scraps) cut into 'wedges' that encircle a contrasting-coloured shape in the centre. The design is then appliquéd to a plain background. It goes without saying that you can create a very colourful block with this method, especially if you use lots of fabrics from your stash.

Various adaptations – for example, stitching different fabrics together first before cutting the wedge shapes – allows a very traditional technique to develop into contemporary designs.

1. Using the templates provided or instructed (we've provided templates for the blocks in our quilt – see pages 169 and 175), cut out the required number of shapes in various colourways. In this example, five different fabrics are used (**Fig. A**) and 20 wedges in total have been cut out.

2. Create the top pointed edge on all wedges: fold each wedge in half widthways, right sides (RS) together, and lightly crease. With a slightly reduced stitch length and ¼in (5mm) seam allowance, machine stitch across the top/widest end (see the purple dashed lines in **Fig. B**) then clip the folded corner at an angle to reduce bulk (**Fig. B**). To speed up this process, you can chain piece these small seams (see page 17 for more information about chain piecing).

3. Turn RS out, ensuring the point is sharp. Centre the point and seam line on the wedge, using the initial crease as your guide. Press; the seam allowance will lie to one side (**Fig. C**). Repeat for all wedges.

4. Return to a regular stitch length. Join the wedges in four groups of five, RS together and ensuring the same colour order (**Fig. D**). Start your stitching ¼in (5mm) down from the top, back-tack up to the top edge, then continue sewing downwards the rest of the seam.

5. Stitch the groups RS together in pairs first, then join the pairs RS together to complete the circle. Pin (or use a spray of fabric adhesive) to position the Dresden 'ring' on your background fabric. To centre your work accurately, you will find it helps to crease your background square in both directions first; you can then position the centre-top, centre-bottom, centre-left and centre-right points of your Dresden 'ring' over the creased marks. Hand appliqué with slip stitch; or, if you prefer, machine appliqué with a straight stitch approximately ⅛in (3mm) all around the outside edge (**Fig. E**).

6. Follow the technique on page 40 to create the centre circle. Make sure the circle is ½in (1.5cm) larger than the centre hole. Centre the circle over the inner raw edges of the Dresden and appliqué as before (**Fig. F**).

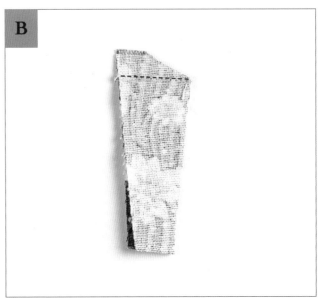

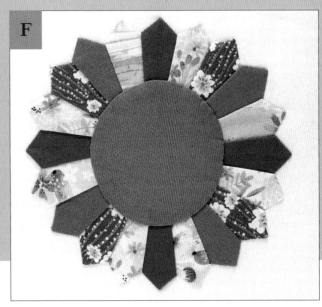

Square within a Square

There are two ways of making this block.

One method (see **Figs. A–C**) is much quicker to create, and you can make the square as large as you want just by adding more squares to each round; however, the points are lost in its creation.

The second method (**Figs. D–F**) leaves you with a sharper finish, and retains the points, but takes a little longer to produce.

METHOD 1

1. Start with two squares of contrasting fabric measuring the same size. Decide which fabric you want as your centre square, and then draw diagonal lines on the wrong side (WS) of the other square (this is your 'border square' fabric). With right sides (RS) together, stitch all around the outside edges with a ¼in (5mm) seam allowance (**Fig. A**).

TIP: If you press your two fabrics together, this will stop them from slipping as you stitch around the outside.

2. Cut along the diagonal lines through the border square fabric only, making sure not to cut the stitching at the corners. Fold and press back the cut edges (be aware these will be on the diagonal, so may distort easily if not pressed correctly). Trim off the 'ears' and square up your block if necessary (**Fig. B**). If you wish, this can be your completed unit.

3. If you wish to increase the size of your block, cut another square of fabric the same size as the square created in Step 2 then repeat the instructions in Steps 1 and 2 (**Fig. C**). Continue in the same way until you reach the size required.

METHOD 2

1. Cut a square for the centre to the size required, and two contrast squares for the 'border triangles' that measure ¼in (5mm) smaller all around. Cut the two contrast squares across the diagonal into four pieces. Mark the centre of one side of the square and the centre of the diagonal edge of one triangle. Matching the centre marks, stitch these two pieces together, fold back and press. Repeat on the opposite side of the square (**Fig. D**).

2. Repeat Step 2 on the remaining two opposite sides. Trim the block if necessary, ensuring a ¼in (5mm) seam allowance, paying particular attention to the seam allowance above the points (**Fig. E**). Rotate the unit by 45 degrees to complete (**Fig. F**).

A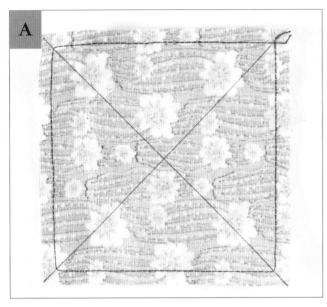

B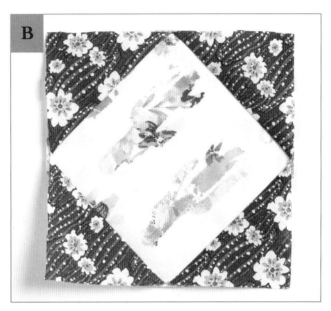

C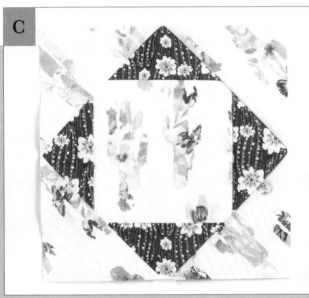

D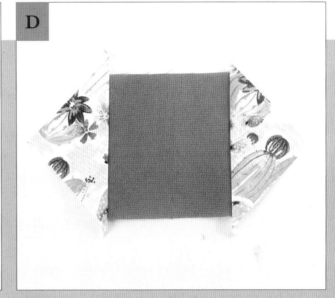

E

F

Curved Piecing

Don't be put off by the thought of curved piecing. By snipping into the seam allowance, and with the aid of a fabric glue pen to hold the curved edges together before stitching, the whole process can be made fairly simple.

If you prefer to pin that's fine; follow the instructions in Step 2, positioning your pins at each end and in the centre of the curve first, then add lots of pins close together in between. Note the points of the pins should be facing outwards. As you stitch along the curve, remove the pins as you go.

For the curved piecing in this book, we will use Drunkard's Path templates (see page 171) – a quarter circle and a background quarter-circle 'frame'. The quarter circle and frame are stitched together along the curved edges to create a square; several of these squares sewn together will produce numerous designs.

1. Start by cutting one of each template in contrasting fabrics (**Fig. A**). Finger-press or mark the centre point on both curved edges. Then make small snips (approximately ½in/1.5cm apart) within the seam allowance, all around the curve of the background frame (white-on-white fabric in the example here).

2. On the right side (RS) of the fabric and within the seam allowance, run your glue pen along the curved edge of the quarter circle. With RS together, lay the background frame over the quarter circle: first match both short ends, followed by the centre points on both pieces, then nudge the curved edge of the background frame into position, ensuring the curved edges match (**Fig. B**). A pair of tweezers will help to manoeuvre the fabric if you need a little help.

3. With the background frame uppermost (but the RS still facing down), machine stitch the two fabrics together with a ¼in (5mm) seam allowance. Avoid making any small tucks in your stitching. Once you have finished sewing the seam, clip through both fabrics where you clipped before and press the seams towards the background. If necessary, trim the unit to the required size, ensuring the background piece along its two straight edges where it meets the curve has a ¼in (5mm) seam allowance (**Fig. C**).

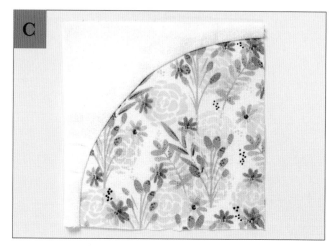

APPLIQUÉ

Appliqué is the method of applying a fabric motif to a quilt or other project. This could be fabric shapes you have cut free-hand or using templates, a hand-stitched shape, or patterns cut from pre-printed fabric.

Because the technique involves sewing a shape onto a background, rather than piecing two fabrics together, it does allow for more complicated shapes to be incorporated into your quilt, and give it more texture too. Bear in mind, however, you'll be sewing around the edge of your shape so the design shouldn't be too intricate – the outline of a hexagon is easier to sew around than a tree!

Applying Shapes in an Order

Before looking at the different appliqué techniques, it's worth highlighting that, for more complex designs, you may need to apply each shape in a particular order to ensure you create an accurate and impactful design.

I. Look at the photographed finished design to start with, and read the instructions closely too.

2. Then, on the background fabric and with the right sides (RS) of the shapes uppermost, start to build up your picture, without attaching anything: place the shapes at the back on the fabric first, then work your way from the background to the foreground shapes. The very foreground shapes should be placed last. Depending on the design, some pieces may overlap each other.

3. Once you've roughly established the order in your mind, and with the photographs of the appliqué block as a reminder, start to press your shapes in place. Again, start with the back piece then work your way towards the foreground, and press each shape for approximately 3 seconds.

If you're attaching multiple shapes and prefer to stitch each shape individually as you go, that's fine. In the example, right, we attached and stitched the bird on the right first, followed by the branch, the second bird's tail, then its body and finally the heart wing.

Where any beginning or finishing stitches will show, pull the threads through to the back and knot off; if the stitches are under another shape, back-tacking to secure threads will be fine.

Raw Edge Appliqué

This technique has become more and more popular in recent years, and is perhaps one of the simplest appliqué techniques. As the name suggests, the raw, unfinished edge of the shape is left visible, becoming a feature in its own right. Using a template or a free-hand drawing, and with the aid of an iron-on adhesive sheet or spray adhesive, the design is adhered to the background fabric. You will then machine stitch around the edge of the design both to secure and embellish the edge of your shape, using a straight, zigzag, satin, blanket or decorative stitch, or free-motion embroidery.

Remember, if you're using a fabric adhesive sheet, the designs will be mirrored once attached to the background fabric.

1. Trace the design onto the smooth/paper side of the fabric adhesive sheet and roughly cut it out, leaving a small ⅛in (3mm) seam allowance all around. Position the cut-out shape on the wrong side (WS) of the desired fabric. With a hot dry iron, press onto the adhesive sheet for approximately 3 seconds (**Fig. A**).

2. Cut out the shape (**Fig. B**). Peel off the paper on the back of the shape – lightly scratching across the back with a pin will help with the removal.

3. Fuse your shape to your background fabric by pressing it in place, the right side (RS) of the shape facing up.

4. Decide which stitch you'll use to appliqué your shapes. We've used a variety in the book, some of which are shown in **Fig. C**. A straight machine stitch should be sewn barely an ⅛in (3mm) from the edge of the shape. A zigzag, satin, blanket or other decorative stitch should cover the raw edge of the shape. (Note: you may need to use sew-in interfacing or thin paper behind the appliqué for satin stitch, to add support.) Free-motion embroidery is usually sewn in a contrasting thread and stitched once or twice around each shape, very close to the edge – don't worry if the second round of stitching doesn't cover the first exactly; the idea is for the stitching to look doodled.

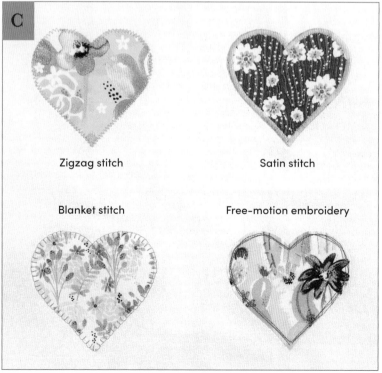

Zigzag stitch

Satin stitch

Blanket stitch

Free-motion embroidery

Needleturn Appliqué

Generally, this is a method of appliqué that involves hand-stitching the shape to the background fabric, turning under the raw edge as you sew your way around the design to create a neat edge. It's not everyone's preference, but it does give the appliqué a more textured finish (as opposed to the flatter finish of raw edge appliqué, detailed opposite), it does not require too much preparation and it is very portable.

Some shapes are notoriously difficult to hand appliqué, and some extra techniques can be used in conjunction to make the process easier and to add structure; these are covered in detail on pages 40–42.

Remember: if your design has several elements, don't forget to look at the design as a whole and appliqué those shapes in the background first (see page 37).

I. Start by tracing your appliqué shape to the right side (RS) of the fabric using a fabric pen. Cut out the shape, adding a scant ¼in (5mm) seam allowance all around. Temporarily secure the shape in position on the background fabric with a dab of glue or a pin. Turn under the seam allowance where you plan to start your stitching by finger-pressing.

Thread a Sharps needle with matching thread. With a knot (or double stitch) on the reverse, bring the needle up close to the turned-under edge. Take the needle down through the background fabric close to where you started. Travel a short way under the fabric before bringing the needle back up along the edge of the appliqué as before, pulling the thread tight. Use the needle tip to turn under the seam allowance ahead of you (**Fig. A**).

If you have a point on your shape, stop sewing a couple of stitches before the point and turn under the seam allowances towards the point and a short way along the next side, ensuring you stitch right into the point. As you work around a curve, tease the seam allowance underneath with the point of your needle; you should not need to clip the seam allowance. If you have an inward point (for example, the indent at the top of the heart), clip into the seam allowance towards the point and, again, encourage the seam allowance under with the tip of your needle.

2. Continue working your way around the whole shape in this way. Finish with a double stitch on the reverse. **Fig. B** shows the completed shape.

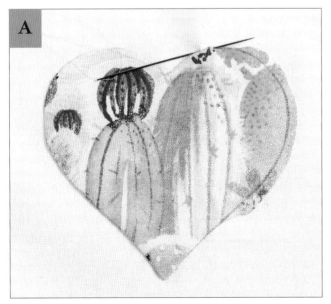

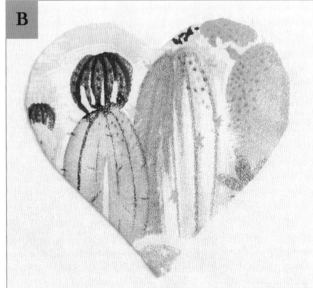

Appliqué with Card

This approach is perfect for circles, since these can get very easily distorted without a sturdy 'lining' to hold their shape.

1. Cut out your circle template from lightweight card and use it to draw a circle on the wrong side (WS) of the appliqué fabric. Set aside the template for the moment. Cut out the circle from fabric, adding a ¼in (5mm) seam allowance all around. With doubled thread and within the seam allowance, sew running stitch around the circle. Make sure to leave a tail of thread at the start and end of the stitching, ideally on the right side (RS) of the fabric (**Fig. A**).

2. Position the card so it's centred on the WS of the fabric circle. Pull the thread tails to gather the seam allowance and wrap it around the card. Ensure the gathers are even then tie off the thread tails with two or three knots (**Fig. B**).

3. Press well on both sides – a spray of starch will help create a crisp crease around the circle edge. Cut the gathering thread, gently remove the card and press again. Appliqué your perfect circle in position by hand or machine (**Fig. C**).

Technique used for the centre of Week 43's block (Small Flower 5). See page 124.

Appliqué with Freezer Paper

With small curved pieces like leaves, or for awkward curves, use freezer paper and starch to achieve the perfect shape.

1. First reproduce your template shape on the dull side of freezer paper. Cut out the shape, along the drawn lines. With the dull side of the shape facing up, press the shiny side to the wrong side (WS) of your appliqué fabric. Cut out the shape, adding a scant ¼in (5mm) seam allowance all around (**Fig. A**).

2. Squirt a little spray starch into the lid of the spray. With a thin paint brush or your finger, apply the starch to the seam allowance. Start at the pointed end of your shape (or any point on your shape if it has multiple points): turn the seam allowance over across the top of the points, then down both sides of the leaf shape while pressing with the tip of your iron; the starch will help adhere the seam allowance to the freezer paper and create a sharp crease around the shape. When the starch has dried, gently remove the freezer paper and press again (**Fig. B**).

3. Appliqué into position by hand or machine (**Fig. C**).

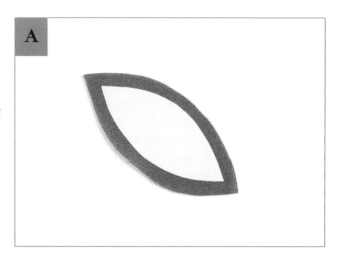

Technique used for Week 38: Heart 8.
See page 114.

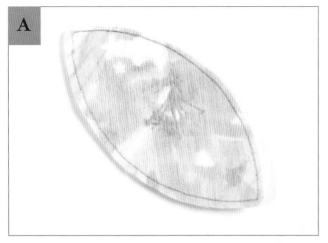

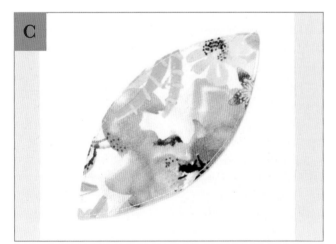

Appliqué with Interfacing

With larger curved pieces, we've use lightweight interfacing to create a perfect curved shape. This can be iron-on or sew-in; you'll just need to make sure the fusible side of the iron-on interfacing is facing the right way.

I. On the non-glue side of iron-on interfacing (or either side of sew-in interfacing), draw around your template. With the right sides (RS) of the fabric and interfacing matching (the fusible side if using iron-on interfacing, either side if using sew-in interfacing), stitch all around the shape along the drawn line. You do not need to leave a gap for turning through. Cut out your shape, adding an ⅛in (3mm) seam allowance all around (**Fig. A**). For such a small seam allowance, you don't need to worry about clipping into the curves; however you should trim across any points. Without cutting into the fabric, carefully cut a small lengthways slit in the back of the interfacing.

2. Turn the shape right side out and then finger-press around the edge (**Fig. B**). If you are using sew-in interfacing, you may wish to press the whole shape; if you are using iron-on interfacing, do not press at this stage.

3. Position the shape in place on the background fabric. If you are using iron-on interfacing, press in place; if you are using sew-in interfacing, you may wish to temporarily secure with a dab of glue or a pin. Appliqué in place by hand or machine (**Fig. C**).

Technique used for Week 24: Tall Flower 2.
See page 92.

Broderie Perse

Broderie Perse is an ancient form of appliqué whereby elements (often flowers and birds) are cut from patterned fabric and 'invisibly' appliquéd onto a background to create a new design. These days, with the use of fabric adhesive sheets, the whole process is really easy.

1. First choose the design elements you wish to use from your patterned fabric. Apply a piece of fabric adhesive sheet behind the design element, on the wrong side (WS) of the fabric, then cut out the design. Use the same process to cut out as many elements necessary to create a new design on your background fabric (**Fig. A**).

2. Arrange the elements on your background fabric, overlapping the shapes where appropriate. Once you're happy with your layout, remove the adhesive sheet backing papers and press the shapes into position. Using a matching or invisible thread, machine appliqué your design onto the background with your chosen stitch (**Fig. B**).

A

B

Technique used for Week 29: Basket 1.
See page 102.

Reverse Appliqué

For this technique, the shape is cut out from the background (top) fabric before adding the appliqué fabric/s from underneath. The reversed design in this example will be a circle, but you could reverse appliqué any shape that's reasonably uncomplicated, such as a heart or large-petalled flower.

I. First decide the finish you want your background (top) fabric to have. Do you want a neater look, with the raw edge of the fabric turned under with hand or machine stitching, or a raw edge appliqué look? In both instances, draw your template shape onto a piece of freezer paper slightly larger than the template and cut out the design. Fuse the shiny side of the template into position on the wrong side (WS) of your background fabric (**Fig. A**).

2. As we're turning under the raw edge in this example, a seam allowance will need to be added to the cut-out shape; you do not need to do this if you're leaving a raw edge on the background (top) fabric. Since we're cutting out a circle for this example, the seam allowance needs to be quite generous. Draw a smaller version of your shape onto the background fabric, approx. ½in (1.5cm) from the edge of the freezer paper inside the hole in the template. Cut out the inner shape – in our case, a smaller circle (**Fig. B**). If your shape has curves like ours, snip into the seam allowance of the inner shape, right up to but not into the freezer paper; this will help you create a neat curve.

3. Squirt a little spray starch into the lid of the spray starch container. With a thin paint brush or your finger, apply the starch to the WS of the seam allowance. Press back the seam allowance over and onto the freezer paper (**Fig. C**).

4. Gently remove the freezer paper then flip the background fabric right side (RS) up. Place your appliqué fabric on the underside of your cut-out shape, RS facing up, ensuring a good seam allowance all around. Pin, baste/tack or glue the appliqué fabric in position then machine or hand appliqué it to the background fabric (**Fig. D**). Trim the excess seam allowance of the appliqué fabric to ¼in (5mm) from the back.

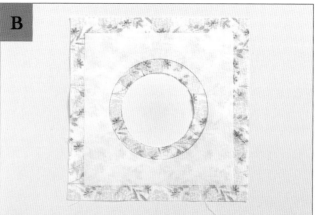

Bias & Straight Strips

Both bias and straight strips are sitting under the 'appliqué' umbrella, as they are used to frame and embolden designs in this book's quilt. Bias strips can be curved easily, and are often used to create movement in flower blocks; straight strips are perfect for flower stems. Bias and straight strips are applied in the same way as the previous appliqué techniques – by hand or by machine.

MAKING BIAS STRIPS

I. Depending on the length of the bias strip required, prepare a piece of fabric which, when measured diagonally, will be long enough. Place your 45-degree line on your ruler on the straight edge of fabric and cut (**Fig. A**).

2. Along the edge just cut, measure the required width of your bias strip (1in or 2.5cm in this case) and cut again (**Fig. B**). Repeat the measuring and cutting strips in the same way.

JOINING STRIPS

If you need to join two strips, place the ends of the strips right sides (RS) together, at right angles to each other, then stitch on the diagonal (**Fig. C**).

ADDING STRIPS TO YOUR BLOCKS

Fold your strip of fabric in half lengthways, wrong sides (WS) together, and press. Unfold the strip, then fold each long edge towards the centre crease, WS together, and press again. Turn the folded strip so the raw edges are at the back, glue the strip into position before appliquéing to the background fabric either by hand or machine – in **Fig. D**, the strips were appliquéd by machine.

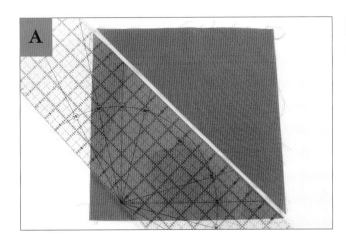

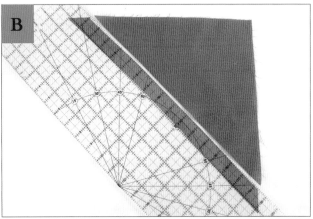

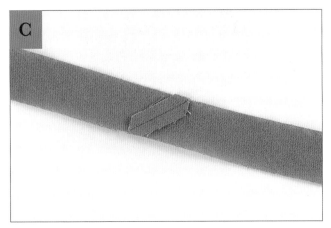

ENGLISH PAPER PIECING

English Paper Piecing (EPP) is a hand-sewn piecing technique used to create often intricate patchwork designs. The shapes are prepared for stitching by folding the fabric over a paper template then glueing or basting/tacking into position. When all the shapes have been prepared, they are then hand-stitched together along the folds using a whip/overcast stitch. On completion, the paper templates are removed (they can be reused several times). Purchased templates made from a special fabric can be left in situ. The most well-known shape for EPP is a hexagon (often called a 'hexie'); however using lots of different shapes can create the most intricate patterns.

By stitching a variety of shapes into one design you can produce amazing patterns, particularly when cutting specific areas of the fabric (known as fussy cutting). In recent years, EPP has become popular with patchworkers since it's extremely portable, no sewing machine is required and it's great if you enjoy stitching in front of the TV!

When it comes to stitching, we prefer to use a slightly longer than average, fine needle, but use whatever needle you're comfortable with. If you're using a fine thread, we recommend knotting this around the needle's eye – this stops the thread from slipping out of the needle, but still allows the needle to run smoothly through the fabric.

ABOVE: Both blocks here are made with English Paper Piecing, and show how complex designs can be. Week 12: Heart 4, above left (see page 70) is a simple yet effective pieced design; Week 19: English Paper Piecing 1, above right (see page 82) is actually simpler than it looks to create, but demonstrates how you can achieve very intricate-looking motifs with clever arrangement.

1. To start, either photocopy or trace the required number of shapes for your design onto paper or lightweight card (or you could recycle waste paper if you have it). It's possible to cut only a limited number of templates and reuse them – see the tip box, at the bottom right of this page, for more information about this.

2. Using the template as your guide, cut out your fabric adding ¼in (5mm) seam allowance around all edges (**Fig. A**).

3. With the wrong side (WS) of the fabric facing you, position the template over the fabric centrally (we like to add a dab of glue to the back of the template to ensure it stays in place, but this is optional). With a fabric glue pen, run a little glue along one edge of either the fabric or the paper then adhere the fabric seam allowance to the template, ensuring a crisp edge. Repeat all the way around the shape, working either clockwise or counterclockwise.

When it comes to corners and points, you may find tweezers useful for making sure these are nice and sharp.

If you prefer to baste/tack the seam allowance down, start in the corner of one edge, fold the seam allowance over the template and baste/tack all the way around the shape, ensuring the corners are stitched securely (**Fig. B**).

Some wrapped shapes will produce 'ears' at the corners, as seen in **Fig. B** – do not cut these off or glue back, just move them out of the way when stitching.

A

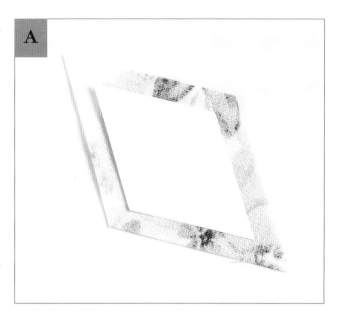

B

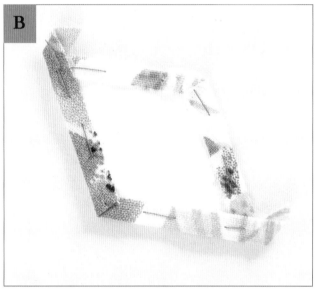

REMOVING TEMPLATES

We like to leave all the templates in place until the design is stitched together; however, this does mean you need to cut the same number of templates as there are fabric shapes. If you wish to reduce the number of templates to cut, you can reuse the papers (and they can be reused several times) for the remaining fabric shapes. Just make sure the shape you are removing the paper from is completely surrounded by and stitched to other shapes (never remove an outside shape until the very end).

C

D

E

4. To stitch your fabric-wrapped pieces together, start by placing two shapes right sides (RS) together. Pass the needle, threaded with matching or neutral-coloured thread (we're deliberately using a darker thread in **Fig. C** for clarity), through the corners of both pieces, catching only a few threads from the folds on each seam allowance. Pull the thread, leaving a short tail. Repeat in the same spot, this time pulling the thread through until you have a loop. Pass your needle through the loop before pulling tight to create a knot. Repeat in exactly the same place for a secure fixing.

You're now ready to proceed along the edge using a whip/overcast stitch. Insert your needle on the opposite side from where it emerged, close to the previous stitch, again catching only a few threads from the folds of each seam allowance as before, and pull tight. Repeat all the way along the edge to the next corner – halfway along, we like to make a knot stitch (as at the start) to help secure the seam.

When you reach the end, make a couple of knot stitches in the same place to finish (**Fig. C**).

5. Continue to join the wrapped pieces as described in the previous step to complete your design. Don't feel you can only stitch one side at a time – if you're adding another shape and can continue stitching without cutting your thread, then do so (we did this for the example in **Fig. D**, where we decided to stitch our six shapes together by sewing two pairs of three units, before stitching the pairs together, as seen in **Fig. E**); however, always make the double-stitch knot described in Step 4 at the beginning and end of each side to secure the stitching. If you need to bend or manipulate your wrapped templates for ease of stitching then that's fine, they'll flatten back into place when your stitching is complete.

6. To remove the template, either unpick the basting/tacking stitches or gently tease the seam allowances around the shape to come away from the paper (sliding a seam ripper/quick unpick gently under the seam allowance is great for this).

7. You're now ready to appliqué your design onto backing fabric either by hand or machine stitching.

FOUNDATION PAPER PIECING

Foundation Paper Piecing (FPP) is a bit like sewing by numbers. You'll be provided with templates in the book to reproduce onto photocopy or tracing paper (or trace onto a fine sew-in interfacing if you prefer); these act as a stabilizer for your fabric pieces. The templates will have a numerical order (and sometimes an alphabetical order – see the third tip in the box, right); these represent the order in which you add and stitch your fabric pieces: first add 1 (or A), then 2 (or B), and so on. Fabrics are positioned on the back of the template then stitched in place from the front, following the printed lines. On completion, the template is removed (if you have used interfacing or stabilizer, this can be left in situ).

All will become clear once you have a go! It takes a bit of mastering but once you've figured it out, it's a relatively easy way to achieve precise points and very accurate blocks. Note that the templates are printed in reverse, so unless the design is symmetrical the finished block will be a mirror image of the template.

NOTES ON FPP

– Fabric cutting details will be given for the FPP patterns in this book, but be aware this technique does tend to use more fabric. So, wherever possible, hold onto and use up your scraps – as you work your way through the quilt, you'll probably collect enough off-cuts to use for FPP blocks!

– When sewing on the fabric pieces, reduce your stitch length to 1.5; this shorter length perforates the paper, and makes it easier to tear it away after the block is completed.

– Blocks for Weeks 25 and 45 in this book (see pages 94 and 126) are sewn in smaller sections first, indicated by letters A, B, C, D, etc. on the template. Follow the general instructions for piecing these individual units; specific details will be given for assembling the blocks.

BELOW: Week 18: Heart 5, left (see page 81) and Week 32: Star 7, right (see page 107), are both made with FPP.

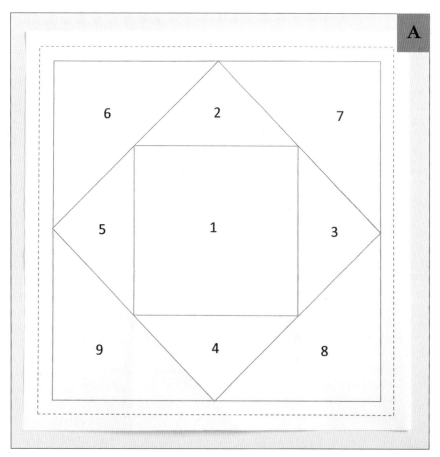

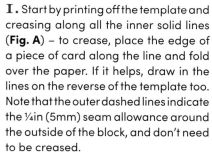

A

6	2	7
5	1	3
9	4	8

I. Start by printing off the template and creasing along all the inner solid lines (**Fig. A**) – to crease, place the edge of a piece of card along the line and fold over the paper. If it helps, draw in the lines on the reverse of the template too. Note that the outer dashed lines indicate the ¼in (5mm) seam allowance around the outside of the block, and don't need to be creased.

2. All cutting amounts given in the patterns are large enough to cover the shapes within the block plus at least a ¼in (5mm) seam allowance all around (seams will subsequently be trimmed to ¼in/5mm). Flip the template (so you can't see the printed lines). With the right side (RS) of the fabric facing up, position your shape 1 fabric piece over the area marked '1', ensuring there's a ¼in (5mm) seam allowance all around – the creases will help indicate the outline of each area. If it helps, hold the template and positioned fabric piece up to a light to check placement. When you're happy, temporarily secure the fabric piece with a pin or a dab of glue (**Fig. B**).

B

3. Flip the template so the printed lines are uppermost. Fold back the crease on the template between areas 1 and 2. Trim the seam allowance of the shape 1 fabric piece to ¼in (5mm) from the paper fold. Flip the template once again, so the back is facing you once more. With the RS of the fabric together, match the edge of the shape 2 fabric piece with the trimmed seam allowance of the shape 1 fabric piece. We like to run a little glue inside the ¼in (5mm) seam line to help hold the two shapes in place, as the template needs to be flipped once more. If you're not sure you've covered all the seam lines, gently fold back the fabric and hold up to the light to check again. Stitch along the printed line. There's no need to reinforce at the start and finish of your stitching and if you go beyond the lines by a stitch or two, don't worry. Flip the fabric over and press away from the centre (**Fig. C**).

4. Repeat Step 3 to add the next piece of fabric between fabric shapes 1 and 3 (**Fig. D**). This time you can also trim the seam allowance across shapes 2 and 3 in readiness for adding shape 7 later.

5. Continue to add the remaining fabric shapes to their corresponding numbers on the paper in numerical order, trimming, glueing and stitching as before, until you've completed the block. When it comes to the shapes that form the outer edges of the blocks, make sure you have at least a ¼in (5mm) seam allowance (indicated by the dashed lines) all around the outer edge so you can accurately trim the block to size (**Fig. E**).

6. When your block is complete, trim the outer seam allowance to ¼in (5mm) before removing the paper. Gently remove the outer shapes first (try not to stretch your stitches), then work inwards until the paper is removed.

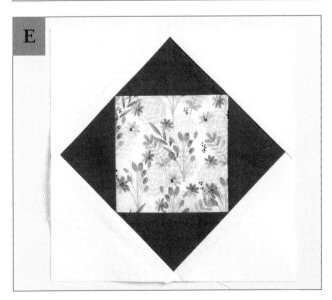

THE
BLOCKS

FLYING GEESE 1

UNFINISHED SIZE
18½ x 6½in (47 x 16.5cm)

TECHNIQUE
Single Flying Geese
(see page 26)

WHAT YOU NEED
▸ Six 6½ x 3½in (16.5 x 9cm) strips in WW
▸ Four 3½in (9cm) squares in Fab D
▸ Four 3½in (9cm) squares in Fab E
▸ Four 3½in (9cm) squares in Fab F

1. Following the technique on page 26, construct two units in each of the three colourways (**Fig. A** shows one unit in Fab D). You should have six units in total.

2. Stitch the units together, with the WW 'geese' pointing in the same direction as shown in the photograph, left.

Week 2
HEART 1

UNFINISHED SIZE
6½in (16.5cm) square

TECHNIQUE
Foundation Paper Piecing (FPP)
(see page 49)

WHAT YOU NEED
▸ Paper
▸ Template (see page 168)
▸ One 4in (10cm) square in WW –
  cut in half across the diagonal
▸ One 3½in (9cm) squar in WW –
  cut in half across the diagonal,
  discard one triangle
▸ One 2½in (6.5cm) squares in WW
  – cut in half across the diagonal
▸ One 6 x 1¾in (15.5 x 4.5cm) strip in Fab B
▸ One 2¾ x 1¾in (7 x 4.5cm) strip in Fab B
▸ One 6 x 1¾in (15.5 x 4.5cm) strip in Fab D
▸ One 2¾ x 1¾in (7 x 4.5cm) strip in Fab D
▸ One 6 x 1¾in (15.5 x 4.5cm) strip in Fab E
▸ One 2¾ x 1¾in (7 x 4.5cm) strip in Fab E

I. Trace off or photocopy the template onto your paper.

2. Referring to the technique on page 49 and with your pattern duly creased, place the 3½in (9cm) size WW triangle in position 1 (note the outside edge will be on the diagonal). Add the shorter D, E and B strips, then the 2½in (6.5cm) WW triangle in position 5 (**Fig. A**).

3. Continue to add the longer strips in the same order, the second 2½in (6.5cm) WW triangle and finally the two 4in (10cm) triangles in the lower corners. Trim to 6½in (16.5cm) square and remove the paper.

A
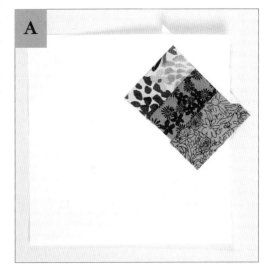

Week 3

STAR 1

UNFINISHED SIZE
6½in (16.5cm) square

TECHNIQUE
Four-in-One Half Square Triangles
(see page 20)

WHAT YOU NEED
▸ Two 4¼in (11cm) squares in WW
▸ One 4¼in (11cm) square in Fab C
▸ One 2½in (6.5cm) square in Fab C
▸ One 4¼in (11cm) square in Fab H

I. Following the technique on page 20, make up a set (four squares) of Half Square Triangles with one 4¼in (11cm) WW square and the 4¼in (11cm) Fab C square, and a set (four squares) of Half Square Triangles with the other 4¼in (11cm) WW square and the 4¼in (11cm) Fab H square. Trim the Half Square Triangles to 2½in (6.5cm) – see **Fig. A**.

2. Assemble the units in three rows:

Rows 1 and 3: Stitch a WW/Fab C unit either side of a WW/Fab H unit, with Fab C in the outer corners.

Row 2: Stitch a WW/Fab H unit either side of the 2½in (6.5cm) Fab C square (**Fig. B**).

3. Stitch the three rows together to complete the block.

ABOVE: Pillow cover, using the
Small Flower 1 design on page 58.

SMALL FLOWER 1

UNFINISHED SIZE
6½in (16.5cm) square

TECHNIQUES
English Paper Piecing (EPP)
(see page 46)

Bias & Straight Strips
(see page 45)

WHAT YOU NEED
▸ Paper or thin card
▸ Templates (see page 169)
▸ One 5¾in (15cm) square in WW
▸ Two 3⅛ x 1½in (8 x 4cm) strips in WW
▸ One 4½ x 1½in (11.5 x 4cm) strip in Fab B
▸ One 3⅞ x 1½in (10 x 4cm) strip in Fab B
▸ One 3½ x 1in (9 x 2.5cm) strip in Fab B
▸ Two 2in (5cm) squares in Fab C
▸ One 2in (5cm) square in Fab D
▸ One 1½in (4cm) square in Fab H

I. To prepare your EPP shapes, copy the templates onto the sheet of paper or thin card. Divide and cut the circle into four equal quarters, then discard one quarter. Follow the EPP instructions on page 46 to prepare and cover the paper shapes. Create the flowerhead by stitching the two Fab C quarter circles either side of the Fab D quarter circle with whip/overcast stitch (if you start at the curved edge, you won't need to cut your thread), then add the Fab H square between the Fab C quarter circles and stitch two sides (**Fig. A**). Press the flowerhead then remove the papers (see also the tip below).

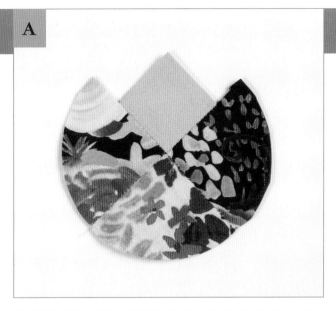

2. With the 3½ x 1in (9 x 2.5cm) Fab B strip, and following the technique on page 45, prepare the flower stem. Appliqué the stem (by hand or machine) on the diagonal into the lower left-hand corner of the 5¾in (15cm) WW square. Position the base of the flowerhead at the top of the stem, covering it slightly and so the Fab H square 'points' towards the top right-hand corner. Pin or glue the flowerhead into position and then appliqué in place either by hand or machine (**Fig. B**).

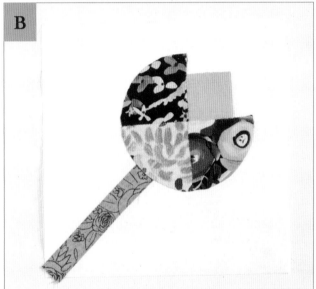

3. To form the outer leaves, measure 1½in (4cm) down on both WW strips and draw a diagonal line on each that points towards a top corner, one piece pointing towards the top-left corner and one pointing towards the top-right corner. With RS facing, place one WW strip over the 3⅞ x 1½in (10 x 4cm) Fab B strip at right angles and stitch along the diagonal line, as indicated by the green dashed line (**Fig. C**). Repeat with the remaining WW strip and the 4½ x 1½in (11.5 x 4cm) Fab B strip, but with the WW strip at a right angle in the opposite direction. Trim seams and press.

4. Stitch the shorter leaf to the lower edge first, then add the remaining leaf to the left edge.

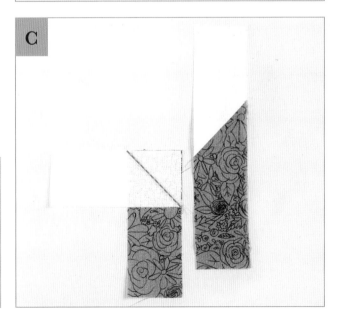

TIP

Before removing the papers, apply a little starch on the outside edges of all the pieces to help retain their shapes.

Week 5

HEART 2

UNFINISHED SIZE
6½in (16.5cm) square

TECHNIQUE
Two-in-One Half Square Triangles
(see page 19)

WHAT YOU NEED
▶ One 4in (10cm) square in WW
▶ Two 2½in (6.5cm) squares in WW
▶ One 4in (10cm) square in Fab A
▶ Two 2½in (6.5cm) squares in Fab C
▶ One 2in (5cm) square in Fab D
▶ One 2in (5cm) square in Fab E
▶ One 2in (5cm) square in Fab F
▶ One 2in (5cm) square in Fab G

I. Construct one large and two smaller sets of Half Square Triangle units, following the technique on page 19. Trim the larger units to 3½in (9cm) square and the smaller units to 2in (5cm) square. Join the four smaller units together for Row 1 and the two large units together for Row 3, rotating the units where necessary to have the arrangement seen in **Fig. A**.

2. Join the four remaining fabric squares together in the following order: F, D, G and E (**Fig. B**); this forms Row 2.

3. Finally, join the three rows together to complete the block.

A

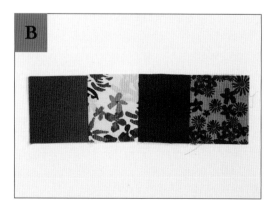

B

Week 6
BIRD 1

TECHNIQUE
Single Flying Geese
(see page 26)

WHAT YOU NEED
▶ Four 2in (5cm) squares in WW
▶ One 5½ x 1½in (14 x 4cm) strip in Fab B
▶ One 4½ x 1½in (11.5 x 4cm) strip in Fab B
▶ One 5½ x 1½in (14 x 4cm) strip in Fab D
▶ One 3½ x 1½in (9 x 4cm) strip in Fab D
▶ One 6½ x 1½in (16.5 x 4cm) strip in Fab E
▶ One 4½ x 1½in (11.5 x 4cm) strip in Fab E
▶ One 3½ x 2in (9 x 5cm) strip in Fab F
▶ One 3½ x 2in (9 x 5cm) strip in Fab G

I. Following the technique on page 26, prepare two Flying Geese units in Fab F/WW and Fab G/WW. Stitch these units together, with the Fab F/WW unit on top (**Fig. A**).

2. Next add the shorter 3½ x 1½in (9 x 4cm) Fab D strip to the lower edge, followed by the 4½ x 1½in (11.5 x 4cm) Fab B strip to the right edge (**Fig. B**).

3. To complete the block, continue adding the remaining strips to the lower and right side edges in the following order: 4½ x 1½in (11.5 x 4cm) in Fab E, 5½ x 1½in (14 x 4cm) in Fab D, 5½ x 1½in (14 x 4cm) in Fab B, and 6½ x 1½in (16.5 x 4cm) in Fab E.

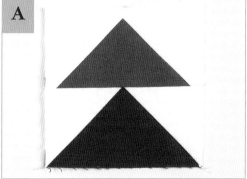

A

B

Week 7
STAR 2

UNFINISHED SIZE
6½in (16.5cm) square

TECHNIQUE
Foundation Paper Piecing (FPP)
(see page 49)

WHAT YOU NEED
▸ Paper
▸ Template (see page 169)
▸ Eight 3¼ x 2¼in (8.5 x 6cm) strips in WW
▸ Four 3 x 1½in (8 x 4cm) strips in WW
▸ Four 4½ x 2¼in (11.5 x 6cm) strips in Fab A
▸ One 1½in (4cm) square in Fab A

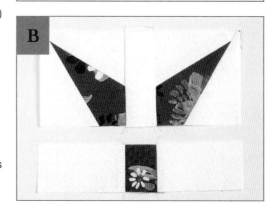

I. Start by making four copies of the small FPP template. Following the technique on page 49, construct a unit with one 4½ x 2¼in (11.5 x 6cm) Fab A strip over position 1 and a 3¼ x 2¼in (8.5 x 6cm) WW strip on either side of it. Repeat to make four identical units in total. Trim to ¼in (5mm) seam allowance around each unit then remove the papers (**Fig. A**).

2. Assemble the units in three rows as follows:

Rows 1 and 3: Stitch two of the FPP units either side of one 3 x 1½in (8 x 4cm) WW strip, along the longest edges of the strip (see top of **Fig. B**).

Row 2: Stitch a 3 x 1½in (8 x 4cm) WW strip either side of the 1½in (4cm) Fab A square (see bottom of **Fig. B**).

3. Rotate Row 3 so the points point downwards. Stitch the three rows together, so that the points face outwards towards the corners.

LOG CABIN 1

UNFINISHED SIZE

12½in (32cm) square

TECHNIQUE

Log Cabin (see page 30) – note: this is a slight variation on the Log Cabin block, although it is made up in a similar way.

WHAT YOU NEED

▶ Four 1½in (4cm) squares in WW
▶ Four 1½ x 2½in (4 x 6.5cm) strips in WW
▶ Four 1½ x 3½in (4 x 9cm) strips in WW
▶ Four 1½ x 4½in (4 x 11.5cm) strips in WW
▶ Four 1½ x 5½in (4 x 14cm) strips in WW
▶ Four 1½ x 6½in (4 x 16.5cm) strips in WW
▶ Four 1½ x 2½in (4 x 6.5cm) strips in Fab C
▶ Four 1½ x 3½in (4 x 9cm) strips in Fab D
▶ Four 1½ x 4½in (4 x 11.5cm) strips in Fab B
▶ Four 1½ x 5½in (4 x 14cm) strips in Fab E
▶ Four 1½in (4cm) squares in Fab H

1. Referring to the technique on page 30, start by joining the Fab H and WW squares. With the Fab H square on the right, add the 1½ x 2½in (4 x 6.5cm) WW rectangle to the lower edge, followed by a 1½ x 2½in (4 x 6.4cm) Fab C rectangle to the right (we're now working in a counter-clockwise direction). Continue to add strips in the following order: 1½ x 3½in (4 x 9cm) in Fab D (square up your block at this point if necessary), 1½ x 3½in (4 x 9cm) in WW, 1½ x 4½in (4 x 11.5cm) in WW, 1½ x 4½in (4 x 11.5cm) in Fab B, 1½ x 5½in (4 x 14cm) in Fab E, 1½ x 5½in (4 x 14cm) in WW, and 1½ x 6½in (4 x 16.5cm) in WW. **Fig. A** shows how the unit looks, once all pieces are stitched together.

2. Repeat Step 1 to make four units in total.

3. Arrange the four units to look like the finished block in the photograph on page 63, rotating the units where necessary so the WW pieces form a 'border' around the outer edge. Stitch the units together in pairs first, then stitch the pairs together to complete the block.

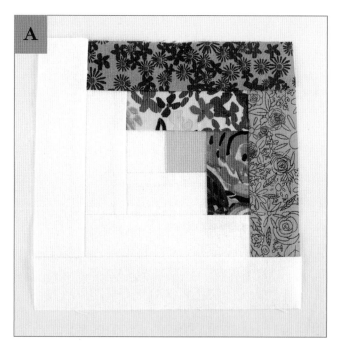

A

Centre-top area of the quilt.

Week 9

CENTRE PANEL 1

UNFINISHED SIZE
24½ x 4½in (62.5 x 11.5cm)

TECHNIQUE
Raw Edge Appliqué
(see page 38)

WHAT YOU NEED
▸ Fabric adhesive sheets
▸ Template (see page 169)
▸ Five 4½ x 2¼in (11.5 x 6cm) strips in WW
▸ Two 4½ x 1¼in (11.5 x 3.5cm) strips in WW
▸ Twelve 3 x 1¼in (8 x 3.5cm) strips in WW
▸ Six 3in (8cm) squares in Fab D
▸ One 9 x 2in (23 x 5cm) strip in Fab F

I. Trace the template onto fabric adhesive sheets. Following the Raw Edge Appliqué technique on page 38, prepare and cut out your heart appliqué shapes using the 9 x 2in (23 x 5cm) Fab F strip. Centre each heart on a Fab D square. Decide which appliqué stitch you wish to use (we used zigzag stitch) and sew all around each individual heart, making six units in total.

2. Add 3 x 1¼in (8 x 3.5cm) WW strips to the left- and right-hand sides of each appliqué unit. Group the six units into two sets, one with three hearts the right way up and one with three hearts upside down. Add a 4½ x 2¼in (11.5 x 3.5cm) WW strip to the top edge of three of the right way up hearts and a 4½ x 2¼in (11.5 x 3.5cm) WW strip to the bottom edge of two upside down hearts (**Fig. A**).

3. Arrange the six units as shown in the photograph of the finished block, left – the three upside-down heart units at the top, and the right-way-round heart units at the bottom. Note the right-way-round heart unit with only the side strips should be at the very bottom, and the upside-down heart with only the side strips should sit above the top right-way-round heart. Sew the units together. Finish the block by stitching a 4½ x 1¼in (11.5 x 3.5cm) strip to the top and bottom ends.

A

HEART 3

UNFINISHED SIZE
6½in (16.5cm) square

TECHNIQUE
Machine Piecing

WHAT YOU NEED
▸ Two 2½in (6.5cm) squares in WW
▸ Four 1in (2.5cm) squares in WW
▸ Two 6½ x 1½in (16.5 x 4cm) strips in Fab A
▸ Two 4½ x 1½in (11.5 x 4cm) strips in Fab A
▸ Two 4½ x 2½in (11.5 x 6.5cm) strips in Fab F

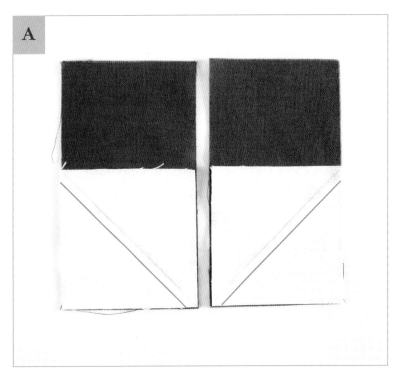

1. First draw a diagonal line on all WW squares. With RS facing, position the larger WW squares on the Fab F strips, matching the side and lower edges, and with the diagonal lines running in opposite directions to form the lower point (**Fig. A**). Stitch along the drawn diagonal lines then trim off the bottom triangles ¼in (5mm) away from the seams (see the pink lines in **Fig. A**). Press the seams open to avoid bulk.

2. Repeat with the smaller squares on both top corners of both strips, this time with the diagonal lines running from the top to the side edges on each piece to form the shaped top. Trim and press the seams as before.

3. With RS facing and matching the seam lines, join the two units to form the heart shape. Again, press the seams open (**Fig. B**).

4. To create the 'frame' around the heart unit, first join the 4½ x 1½in (11.5 x 4cm) Fab A strips to the top and lower edges, followed by the two 6½ x 1½in (16.5 x 4cm) Fab A strips on each side.

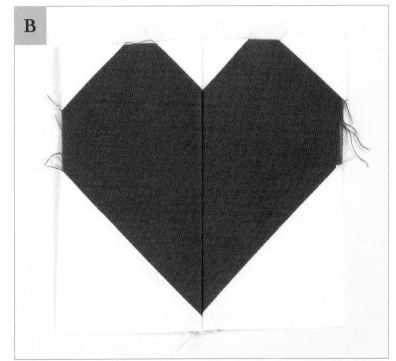

Week 11

LARGE PIECED BLOCK 1

UNFINISHED SIZE
12½in (32cm) square

TECHNIQUES
Four-in-One Half Square Triangles
(see page 20)

Split Half Square Triangles
(see page 22)

Checkerboard – Four Patch
(see page 29)

WHAT YOU NEED
▶ One 7¼in (18.5cm) square in WW
▶ One 4½in (11.5cm) square in WW
▶ One 7¼in (18.5cm) square in Fab D
▶ Eight 2½in (6.5cm) squares in Fab D
▶ Eight 2½in (6.5cm) squares in Fab E
▶ Four 4½in (11.5cm) squares in Fab H

I. The Split Half Square Triangle units in this block are identical. Using the 7¼in (18.5cm) WW square and 7¼in (18.5cm) Fab D square, and following the technique on page 20, create four Half Square Triangles. Trim the units to 4½in (11.5cm) square if necessary. Next, with the 4½in (11.5cm) Fab H contrast square, continue with Steps 2 and 3 of the Split Half Square Triangle technique on page 22 to create four identical units that look like **Fig. A**.

2. Following the technique on page 29, create four four-patch units in Fab D and E (**Fig. B**).

3. Assemble the units in three rows as follows:

Rows 1 and 3: Stitch a Four Patch Checkerboard unit either side of a Split Half Square Triangle unit (see top of **Fig. C**).

Row 2: Stitch a Split Half Square Triangle unit either side of the 4½in (11.5cm) WW square, with the Fab D triangles on outer edges (see bottom of **Fig. C**).

4. Rotate Row 3 by 180 degrees, so the Fab D triangle is on the bottom. Stitch the three rows together to complete the block.

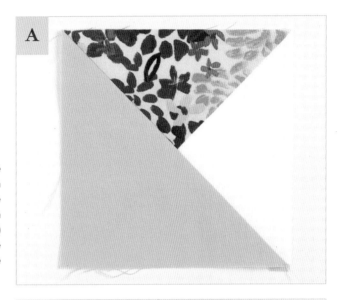

A

B

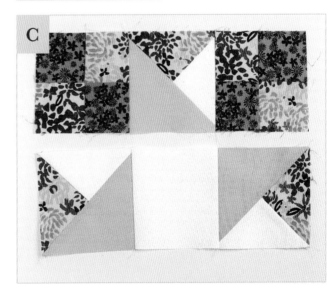

C

HEART 4

UNFINISHED SIZE
6½in (16.5cm) square

TECHNIQUES
English Paper Piecing (EPP)
(see page 46)

Appliqué

WHAT YOU NEED
▸ Paper or thin card

▸ Template (see page 169)

▸ One 6½in (16.5cm) square in WW

▸ One 2in (5cm) square in each pattern
and plain fabric (Fab A–H)

1. Prepare your EPP shapes: trace the 2¾in (7cm) circle template onto the paper or thin card twice, then divide and cut each circle into four equal quarters. Following the EPP instructions on page 46, prepare and cover the eight paper shapes with each plain and patterned fabric.

2. Using whip/overcast stitch and referring to **Fig. A**, join the quarter circles: first join the Fab E and Fab F quarter circles along two straight edges, from the top curve downwards, to form a semi-circle. Without cutting your thread, and with the curved edge pointing downwards, sew the Fab B quarter circle unit to the remaining straight edge of Fab E. Without cutting the thread again, and with the curved edge pointing upwards, sew the Fab C quarter circle to the remaining straight edge of Fab B. Not cutting the thread, and with the curved edge pointing to the right, sew the Fab G quarter circle to the remaining straight edge of Fab C. Fasten off the thread.

3. With the same method, add the Fab A quarter circle to the remaining straight edge of the Fab F unit, with the curved edge pointing to the right/inwards. Repeat on the other side of the heart with Fab D and Fab G units, this time the curved edge of Fab D pointing to the left/inwards.

4. Press the joined shapes then remove the papers (**Fig. B**). Spraying a little starch on the outside edges of all pieces (but particularly the curves) will help retain the overall shape before removing the papers.

5. Position the joined shapes on the RS of the WW square, with the top of the curve approx. 1⅛in (approx. 3cm) down from the top, and the side curves ⅞in (approx. 2.5cm) in from each side. Pin or glue in place. Add the final Fab H quarter circle between the bottom tips of the Fab A and D quarter circles, its curved edge pointing up/inwards then appliqué in place by hand or machine.

A

B

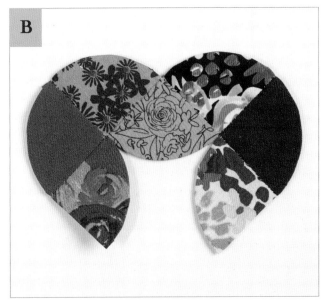

Week 13
STAR 3

UNFINISHED SIZE
6½in (16.5cm) square

TECHNIQUE
Foundation Paper Piecing (FPP)
(see page 49)

WHAT YOU NEED
▸ Paper
▸ Template (see page 169)
▸ Two 4in (10cm) squares in WW –
  cut each in half diagonally to
  produce four pieces
▸ Two 4in (10cm) squares in Fab E –
  cut each in half diagonally to
  produce four pieces
▸ Four 3¾in x 2in (9.5 x 5cm) strips
  in Fab H

I. Start by making four copies of the FPP template. Following the technique on page 49, on one copy of the template place a WW triangle over position 1, then add the Fab H strip on position 2, and lastly add the Fab E triangle on position 3. Trim to ¼in (5mm) seam allowance around each unit and remove the papers (**Fig. A**). Repeat to make four units in total.

2. Arrange the units as shown in the photograph of the finished block above, rotating them as necessary. Sew the units together in pairs first, then join the pairs to complete the block.

Week 14
BIRD 2

UNFINISHED SIZE
6½in (16.5cm) square

TECHNIQUES
Log Cabin
(see page 30)

Single Half Square Triangle
(see page 19)

WHAT YOU NEED
▸ One 2½in (6.5cm) square in WW
▸ One 2½ (6.5cm) square in Fab B
▸ One 3½ x 1½in (9 x 4cm) strip in Fab A
▸ One 4½ x 1½in (11.5 x 4cm) strip in Fab A
▸ One 5½ x 1½in (14 x 4cm) strip in Fab C
▸ One 6½ x 1½in (16.5 x 4cm) strip in Fab C
▸ One 4½ x 1½in (11.5 x 4cm) strip in Fab D
▸ One 5½ x 1½in (14 x 4cm) strip in Fab D
▸ One 2½ x 1½in (6.5 x 4cm) strip in Fab E
▸ One 3½ x 1½in (9 x 4cm) strip in Fab E
▸ Four 2½in (6.5cm) squares in Fab H

I. Create a Single Half Square Triangle unit with the 2½in (6.5cm) WW and Fab B squares, following the technique on page 19. Rotate the unit so the WW triangle is in the top-left corner. Stitch the 2½ x 1½in (6.5 x 4cm) Fab E strip to the left-hand edge of the Half Square Triangle unit. Press all seams away from the Half Square Triangle unit. Add the 3½ x 1½in (9 x 4cm) Fab E strip to the top of the unit (see top unit in **Fig. A**).

2. To add the 'geese', on the WS of a 2½in (6.5cm) Fab H square draw a diagonal line from top right to bottom left. With RS facing, lay this square over the Half Square Triangle unit, matching the top and side edges. Stitch along the diagonal. Trim the seam allowance to ¼in (5mm), then press the seam away from the Half Square Triangle (see the bottom unit in **Fig. A**).

3. To start the next row, join the two Fab A strips (adding the shorter strip first to the left side) and a 2½in (6.5cm) Fab H square as outlined in Steps 1 and 2 above. Continue building up the final two rows in the same way, ending with the Fab C fabric strips.

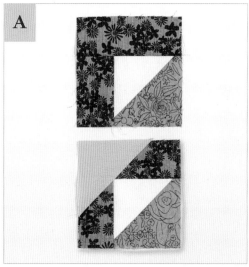

A

73

Week 15

DRESDEN 1

UNFINISHED SIZE

12½in (32cm) square

TECHNIQUES

Dresden Plate
(see page 32)

Appliqué with Card
(see page 40)

Appliqué with Interfacing
(see page 42)

WHAT YOU NEED

▶ Paper

▶ Templates (see page 169)

▶ One 24 x 2in (61 x 5cm) strip in WW

▶ One 12½in (32cm) square in WW

▶ One 4¼in (11cm) square in Fab A

▶ One 24 x 2½in (61 x 6.5cm) strip in Fab F

▶ One 24 x 4in (61 x 10cm) strip in Fab D
(or 17 x 4in/43.5 x 10cm if your fabric is
plain or non-directional)

I. Stitch the WW and Fab F strips together along the longest edges and press the seam open. Trace the wedge template provided onto paper or thin card. With the Fab F section at the bottom, cut 10 wedge shapes from the joined strip. With the same template, also cut 10 wedges from Fab D (if you are using a plain/non-directional fabric, you can top and tail the template). To create the points on the wedges, follow the instructions in Steps 2 and 3 of the Dresden Plate technique (see page 32). **Fig. A** shows the finished wedges.

A

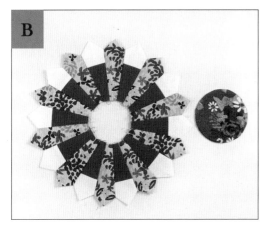

B

2. Arrange the wedges into the 'plate', alternating the two colourways. Stitch the wedges together, first in pairs, then in groups of four, then the whole 'plate'. Following either the technique on page 40 or the technique on page 42, make up centre circle using the Fab A square and circle template (**Fig. B**).

3. Centre the 'plate' on the 12½in (32cm) WW square then appliqué by hand or machine. Finish the block by appliquéing the centre circle in the same way.

Top-left area of the quilt.

STAR 4

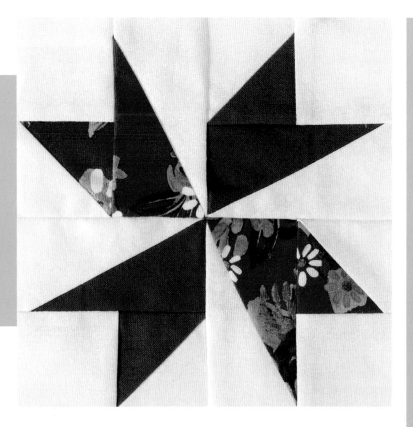

UNFINISHED SIZE
6½in (16.5cm) square

TECHNIQUES
Half Rectangle Triangles
(see page 24)

Two-in-One Half Square Triangles
(see page 19)

WHAT YOU NEED
▶ Paper
▶ Freezer paper
▶ Two 5 x 3in (13 x 8cm) strips in WW
▶ Two 2½in (6.5cm) squares in WW
▶ Four 2in (5cm) squares in WW
▶ One 5 x 3in (13 x 8cm) strip in Fab A
▶ One 2½in (6.5cm) square in Fab A
▶ One 5 x 3in (13 x 8cm) strip in Fab F
▶ One 2½in (6.5cm) square in Fab F

1. Following the technique on page 24, create a 3 x 1½in (8 x 4cm) rectangle template with an 'X' drawn on it, the lines of which run from corner to corner (**Fig. A**).

2. Create two identical Half Rectangle Triangles in both Fab A/WW and Fab F/WW colourways, following the technique on page 24. Following the technique on page 19, construct two identical Half Square Triangle sets in the same colourways (**Fig. B**). Trim the Half Square Triangle sets to 2in (5cm) square if necessary.

3. To create one unit, stitch a 2in (5cm) WW square to the top edge of a Half Square Triangle (the seam line of the Half Square Triangle should run from top left to bottom right) then sew a Half Rectangle Triangle to the right of these joined pieces (its seam running from top left to bottom right). Create a second identical unit in the same colourway, and two identical units in the second colourway.

4. Arrange the units to create the layout seen in the photograph of the finished block opposite, rotating units where necessary. Sew two contrasting colourways in pairs together first (**Fig. C**), then sew the pairs together to complete the block.

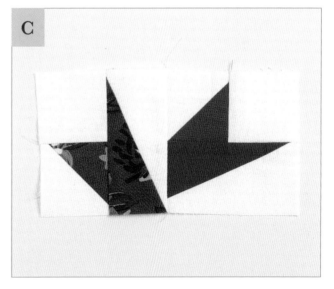

TALL FLOWER 1

UNFINISHED SIZE
18½ x 6½in (47 x 16.5cm)

TECHNIQUES
Checkerboard – Four Patch
(see page 29)

Two-in-One Half Square Triangles
(see page 19)

Four-in-One Half Square Triangles
(see page 20)

Bias & Straight Strips
(see page 45)

WHAT YOU NEED
▶ Two 1½in (4cm) squares in WW
▶ Two 1½in (4cm) squares in Fab D
▶ Three 2½in (6.5cm) squares in WW
▶ Two 1¾in (4.5cm) squares in WW
▶ Two 1¾in (4.5cm) squares in Fab E
▶ Two 3 x 2¼in (8 x 6cm) strips in WW
▶ Six 2in (5cm) squares in WW
▶ Four 2in (5cm) squares in Fab F
▶ Three 6½ x 2in (16.5 x 5cm) strips in WW
▶ Two 3½in (9cm) squares in WW
▶ One 3½in (9cm) square in Fab B
▶ One 2½in (6.5cm) square in Fab B
▶ One 3½ x 1½in (9 x 4cm) strip in WW
▶ One 3½ x 2½in (9 x 6.5cm) strip in WW
▶ One 8¼ x 1in (21 x 2.5cm) strip in Fab B

I. Following the Four Patch Checkerboard technique on page 29, make the three individual flowerhead units as follows:

Top Unit – sew a four-patch unit with the two 1½in (4cm) WW squares and the two 1½in (4cm) Fab D squares. Stitch a 2½in (6.5cm) WW square either side of this four-patch unit.

Middle Unit – sew a four-patch unit with the two 1¾in (4.5cm) WW squares and the two 1¾in (4.5cm) Fab E squares. Stitch a 3 x 2¼in (8 x 6cm) WW strip either side of the checkerboard.

Bottom Unit – sew a four-patch unit with two 2in (5cm) WW squares and two 2in (5cm) Fab F squares. Repeat to make another WW/Fab F four-patch unit. Join the two four-patch units together then stitch a 6½ x 2in (16.5 x 5cm) WW strip either side of the checkerboard.

Stitch these three sections together to form the flowerhead (**Fig. A**).

2. For the leaves, create six Half Square Triangles in Fab B and WW:

Four leaves with the **Four-in-One Half Square Triangles** technique (see page 20) – use one 3½in (9cm) WW square and one 3½in (9cm) Fab B square.

Two leaves with the **Two-in-One Half Square Triangles** technique (see page 19) – use one 2½in (6.5cm) WW square and one 2½in (6.5cm) Fab B square.

Trim all units to 2in (5cm) if necessary.

Continued > > >

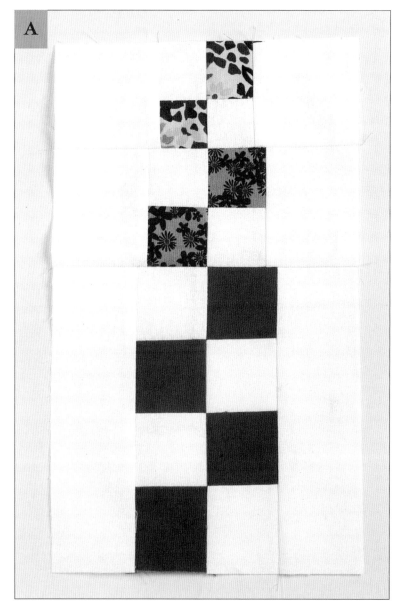

A

3. To make the left-hand side leaf section, stitch two Half Square Triangles together with the Fab B fabrics at the bottom and pointing from the bottom edge inwards. Stitch a Half Square Triangle – with the diagonal running from top left to bottom right – to the right-hand edge of a 2in (5cm) WW square, then join this to the bottom of the stitched pair of Half Square Triangles. Add a 3½ x 1½in (9 x 4cm) WW strip to the top of this unit, and a 3½ x 2½in (9 x 6.5cm) WW strip to the bottom of the unit (**Fig. B**).

4. To make the leaf section on the right-hand side, stitch two Half Square Triangles together with both diagonals running from bottom left to top right: the left-hand Half Square Triangle should have Fab B in the bottom-right corner, and the right-hand Half Square Triangle should have Fab B in the top-left corner. Stitch a 2in (5cm) WW square to the right-hand side of the remaining Half Square Triangle, its Fab B in the top-left corner. Sew this unit to the bottom of the stitched pair of Half Square Triangles. Join a 3½in (9cm) WW square to the top of the unit (**Fig. C**).

5. Join the two units made in Steps 2–4 together. Press the seam open. Add a 6½ x 2in (16.5 x 5cm) WW strip to the bottom of the leaf section. Follow the Bias & Straight Strips technique on page 45, make a stem with the 8¼ x 1in (21 x 2.5cm) Fab B strip. Place the stem down the middle of the leaf section, covering the seam line, then top-stitch in place along the longest edges. To complete the block, join the flowerhead unit to the top of the leaf section.

Week 18
HEART 5

TECHNIQUE
Foundation Paper Piecing (FPP)
(see page 49)

WHAT YOU NEED
▸ Paper

▸ Template (see page 170)

Note: As this block is made up of several small pieces, the cutting instructions are listed in the template placement order. Check your scraps as some may be suitable sizes.

▸ **Position 1:** One 2¼in (6cm) square in WW

▸ **2:** One 2 x 1¼in (5 x 3.5cm) strip in Fab C

▸ **3:** One 3½ x 2¼in (9 x 6cm) strip in Fab F

▸ **4:** One 3¼ x 1¾in (8.5 x 4.5cm) strip in Fab D

▸ **5:** One 2¾ x 1¾in (7 x 4.5cm) strip in Fab H

▸ **6:** One 2¾ x 1½in (7 x 4cm) strip in Fab A

▸ **7 & 15:** One 2in (5cm) square in WW

▸ **8:** One 6½ x 1½in (16.5 x 4cm) strip in Fab G

▸ **9:** One 6¼ x 2¼in (16 x 6cm) strip in Fab B

▸ **10:** One 6¼ x 1¾in (16 x 4.5cm) strip in Fab H

▸ **11:** One 6 x 2¾in (15.5 x 7cm) strip in Fab C

▸ **12:** One 4½ x 2in (11.5 x 5cm) strip in Fab F

▸ **13:** One 3¾ x 1¾in (9.5 x 4.5cm) strip in Fab A

▸ **14:** One 3¾ x 2in (9.5 x 5cm) strip in Fab G

▸ **16 & 17:** One 5 x 3¾in (13 x 5cm) strip in WW

1. Trace off or photocopy the template onto your paper.

2. Cut across the diagonal on the 2¼in (6cm) WW square and discard one half. Add each fabric piece in the order in the list, right, and on the template (short side first). Cut and press the seam allowance as you go. You'll need to cut the 2in (5cm) WW square in half diagonally for positions 7 and 15, placing the diagonals on the seam lines across 3–7 and 9–15.

3. To complete the block, cut the WW rectangle for positions 16 and 17 in half diagonally then place the diagonal cuts either side of the heart.

ENGLISH PAPER PIECING 1

UNFINISHED SIZE
12½in (32cm) square

TECHNIQUES
English Paper Piecing (EPP)
(see page 46)

WHAT YOU NEED

▶ Paper or thin card

▶ Templates (see page 170)

▶ One 12½in (32cm) square in WW

▶ Two 1¼in (3.5cm) wide strips across width of Fab A

▶ One 1½in (4cm) wide strip across width of Fab B

▶ Nine 1½in (4cm) squares in Fab F

I. Start by reproducing the templates provided in paper or thin card – you'll need twelve 2½in (6.5cm) octagons and nine 1in (2.5cm) squares.

2. Stitch the two Fab A strips either side of the Fab B strip, along their longest edges, then press the seams open. Cut the joined strips into twelve 3in (8cm) units.

3. Following the EPP technique on page 46, wrap and secure each of the twelve units around the octagon paper shapes. You'll need to trim the seam allowance to ¼in (5mm) on the diagonal sides of the octagons before securing the fabric to the paper. Pay particular attention to the seam lines made in Step 2, from joining the strips: there's more bulk in these sections, so ensure you create sharp points as you turn the corners under. Using the same EPP technique, wrap and secure the Fab F squares around the square paper shapes (**Fig. A**).

4. Take two octagons and rotate them until the Fab B stripes are vertical. Stitch a square shape in between the two octagons (**Fig. B**). Repeat to make three joined units in total; these will be used for Rows 1, 3 and 5 of the block.

5. Take three octagons and rotate them so the Fab B stripes are horizontal. Stitch the three octagon shapes together, with two square shapes in between them (**Fig. C**). Repeat to make two joined units in total; these will be used for Rows 2 and 4.

6. To assemble the complete design, stitch Rows 1 and 2 together, then stitch Rows 3 and 4, using whip/overcast stitch throughout. Sew the two sets of rows together, then add Row 5 to Row 4. To complete the design, sew the remaining square shapes to either end of Row 3. When all shapes are secured, carefully remove the papers, paying particular attention to the outside edges. Press.

7. Using spray adhesive (or pins), centre the design diagonally onto the 12½in (32cm) WW square. Appliqué in place by hand or machine, around the outside edge.

A

B

C
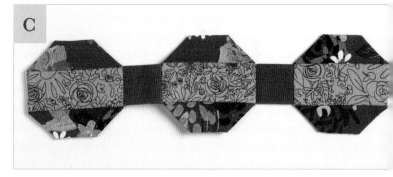

SMALL FLOWER 2

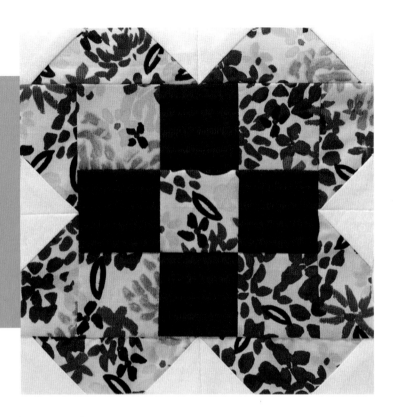

UNFINISHED SIZE
6½in (16.5cm) square

TECHNIQUES
Checkerboard – Nine Patch
(see page 29)

WHAT YOU NEED
▸ Twelve 1¼in (3.5cm) squares in WW –
  mark a diagonal line on the WS of
  all squares
▸ Two 4 x 2in (10 x 5cm) strips in Fab D
▸ Four 3½ x 1¼in (9 x 3.5cm) strips in Fab D
▸ Four 2¾ x 1¼in (7 x 3.5cm) strips in Fab D
▸ One 2in (5cm) square in Fab D
▸ One 4 x 2in (10 x 5cm) strip in Fab G
▸ Two 2in (5cm) squares in Fab G

I. Following the technique on page 29 and using the two 2in (5cm) Fab G squares, one 2in (5cm) Fab D square, two 4 x 2in (10 x 5cm) Fab D strips and one 4 x 2in (10 x 5cm) Fab G strip, create a nine-patch checkerboard, with Fab D as the main fabric and Fab G the contrast (**Fig. A**).

2. Position a WW square over both ends of one 3½ x 1¼in (9 x 3.5cm) Fab D strip, RS facing and with the diagonals running from top centre towards the bottom outer corners. Sew along the diagonal lines then trim the diagonal seam allowances to ¼in (5mm). Repeat to make four units in total. Join two units together (**Fig. B**). Repeat to make a second identical unit.

3. Position a WW square over the right-hand end of a 2¾ x 1¼in (7 x 3.5cm) Fab D strip, RS facing and with the diagonal running from top right to centre bottom. Sew along the diagonal line then trim the diagonal seam to ¼in (5mm). Repeat the process with another 2¾ x 1¼in (7 x 3.5cm) Fab D strip and WW square, this time placing the square over the left-hand end of the strip and with the diagonal running from top left to centre bottom. Once you have the two units, join them together with the WW triangles in the middle (**Fig. C**). Repeat Step 3 to create a second identical unit.

4. To assemble the block, join the units made in Step 3 to each side of the nine-patch checkerboard unit, then add the units made in Step 2 to the top and bottom edges.

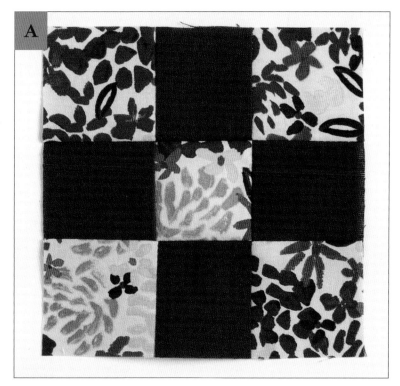

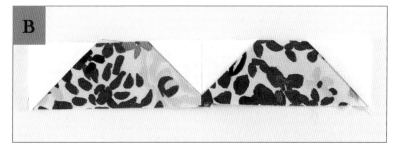

Week 21

SMALL FLOWER 3

UNFINISHED SIZE
6½in (16.5cm) square

TECHNIQUE
Checkerboard – Four Patch
(see page 29)

WHAT YOU NEED
▶ Four 3½in (9cm) squares in WW
▶ Two 3½in (9cm) squares in Fab A
▶ Two 3½in (9cm) squares in Fab C
▶ One 4in (10cm) square in Fab F

1. Fold the WW squares in half along the diagonal and press. Position a folded WW piece over one corner of each Fab A and Fab C square then pin or glue into position. Arrange the Fab A and Fab C squares so they alternate, and so the WW pieces point inwards (**Fig. A**).

2. Stitch the units together in pairs then stitch the pairs together (**Fig. B**). Press the seams open. Note the folded edges of the WW pieces are left unstitched.

3. Centre the Fab F square on top of the WW triangles. Fold the edges of the WW pieces over the edges of the Fab F square to create a curved border. Temporarily secure the folded edges with pins or a glue pen. Stitch down the curved border either by hand with slip stitch or by machine with edge-stitch, making sure you use a matching thread.

Bottom-right area of the quilt.

TALL BIRD 1

UNFINISHED SIZE
18½ x 6½in (47 x 16.5cm)

TECHNIQUE
Raw Edge Appliqué
(see page 38)

WHAT YOU NEED
▸ Fabric adhesive sheets
▸ Templates (see page 171)
▸ 18½ x 6½in (47 x 16.5cm) strip of WW
▸ One 5 x 3in (13 x 8cm) strip in Fab A
▸ One 5 x 3in (13 x 8cm) strip in Fab B
▸ One 5 x 3in (13 x 8cm) strip in Fab C
▸ One 5 x 3in (13 x 8cm) strip in Fab D
▸ One 5 x 3in (13 x 8cm) strip in Fab E
▸ One 3 x 2½in (8 x 6.5cm) strip in Fab A
▸ One 3 x 2½in (8 x 6.5cm) strip in Fab D
▸ One 3 x 2½in (8 x 6.5cm) strip in Fab F
▸ One 3 x 2½in (8 x 6.5cm) strip in Fab G
▸ One 3 x 2½in (8 x 6.5cm) strip in Fab H
▸ Five 1¼ x 1in (3.5 x 2.5cm) strips in Fab H

I. Trace the templates onto fabric adhesive sheets. Following the technique on page 38 and referring to the photograph of the finished block opposite for guidance if necessary, prepare your appliqué shapes – use the larger 5 x 3in (13 x 8cm) strips for the bird bodies, the medium 3 x 2½in (8 x 6.5cm) strips for the wings, and the small 1¼ x 1in (3.5 x 2.5cm) strips for the beaks.

2. Arrange your bird appliqué shapes at slightly jaunty angles over the 18½ x 6½in (47 x 16.5cm) WW strip, referring to the photograph of the finished block on page 88. We left approx. ¼in (5mm) gaps between birds 2–3 and 4–5 (if you are counting from the top down), but you could overlap your birds if you wish. We positioned the top of the top bird body (where it meets the beak) approx. 2½in (6.5cm) down from the top edge, ¾in (2cm) in from the left-hand side and 1¼in (3.5cm) in from the right-hand side. The wings for the birds should sit with the pointed ends pointing towards the body, with the top rounded edges approx. 1¼in (3.5cm) above the top edge of the bird bodies. If you choose to make this block your own and position the birds differently, it's important that you leave at least ½in (1.5cm) margin on both long sides of the background fabric to ensure you don't lose any of the bird features in the seam allowances.

3. To stitch on your appliqué shapes, begin by securing the upper edges of the wings only by pressing them into position. For each bird (we worked from the top down), move the lower part of the wing out the way while stitching the bird body (we stitched blanket stitch all around by machine, starting from under the wing). Once the body is stitched, press the lower part of the wing into position and stitch around the whole wing, using the same stitch and starting at the lower point. Lastly, add the beak at a slight downward angle, butting it up against the bird body – this time we used machine satin stitch (**Fig. A**).

STAR 5

UNFINISHED SIZE
6½in (16.5cm) square

TECHNIQUE
Four-in-One Half Square Triangles
(see page 20)

WHAT YOU NEED

▸ One 3½in (9cm) square in WW

▸ One 3½in (9cm) square in Fab G

▸ Two 3½ x 2in (9 x 5cm) strips in Fab B

▸ Two 3½ x 2in (9 x 5cm) strips in Fab D

▸ Eight 2in (5cm) squares in WW

1. Following the Four-in-One Half Square Triangle technique on page 20, create four identical Fab G/WW units using the 3½in (9cm) WW and Fab G squares. Trim all units to 2in (5cm) square if necessary.

2. Draw a diagonal line on the WS of four of the 2in (5mm) WW squares. Position one of these WW squares on top of a Fab B strip, with the diagonal running from top right to bottom left. Stitch along the diagonal line, trim the seam allowance to ¼in (5mm) then press. Repeat on the second Fab B strip and the two Fab D strips (**Fig. A**).

3. This block is assembled in four quarter units. Join a 2in (5cm) WW square to the left-hand side of a Half Square Triangle unit (with the Fab G triangle in the bottom-left corner). Sew the Fab B/WW unit made in Step 2 to the bottom edge of the Half Square Triangle/WW unit. Repeat to make a second identical unit, and two units in the Fab D colourway (**Fig. B**).

4. Arrange the four quarter units in the layout shown in the photograph of the finished block opposite, rotating units where necessary. Stitch the quarter units in pairs, then stitch the pairs together to complete the block.

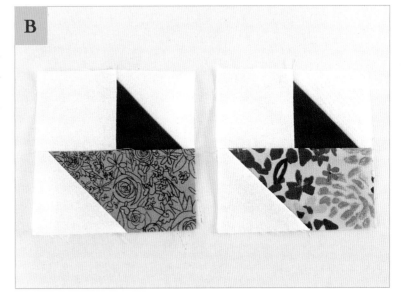

TALL FLOWER 2

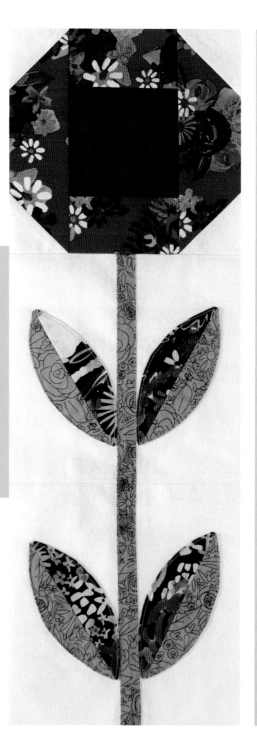

UNFINISHED SIZE
18½ x 6½in (47 x 16.5cm)

TECHNIQUES
Appliqué with Interfacing
(see page 42)

Bias & Straight Strips
(see page 45)

WHAT YOU NEED
▸ Template (see page 174)
▸ Four 2in (5cm) squares in WW
▸ Two 6½in (16.5cm) squares in WW
▸ Two 6½ x 2in (16.5 x 5cm) strips in Fab A
▸ Two 3½ x 2in (9 x 5cm) strips in Fab A
▸ One 12½ x 1in (32 x 2.5cm) strip in Fab B
▸ One 9½ x 1½in (23 x 4cm) strip in Fab B
▸ One 9½ x 1½in (23 x 4cm) strip in Fab C
▸ One 3½in (9cm) square in Fab G
▸ One 9 x 2¼in (23 x 6cm) strip of iron-on
  or sew-in interfacing

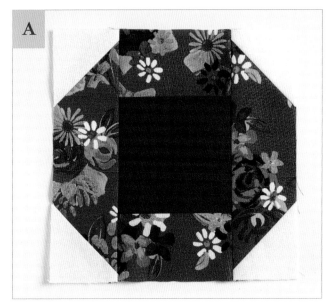

A

1. Start by drawing a diagonal line on the WS of the four 2in (5cm) WW squares. Position two of these at either end of a 6½ x 2in (16.5 x 5cm) Fab A strip, RS facing, with the WW triangles on the top outer corners and ensuring the diagonals run from top centre to bottom outer. Stitch along the diagonals, trim the seam allowance to ¼in (5mm) then press. Repeat to make a second identical unit.

2. Stitch the 3½ x 2in (9 x 5cm) Fab A strips to the top and bottom of the 3½in (9cm) Fab G square. Stitch the units made in Step 1 to each side of the Fab G square unit, with the WW triangles on the outer corners (**Fig. A**).

3. To make the leaves, first stitch the two 9½ x 1½in (23 x 4in) Fab B and Fab C strips together along their length then press the seams open. Transfer the template onto the interfacing. Following the technique on page 42, create four identical leaf shapes (**Fig. B**).

4. Following the technique on page 45, make a straight stem with the 12½ x 1in (32 x 2.5cm) Fab B strip.

5. Join the two 6½in (16.5cm) WW squares. Top-stitch the stem piece from Step 4 over the seam of the joined WW squares. Position the leaves either side of the stem, two leaves sitting 1in (2.5cm) above the middle seam line and the two remaining leaves sitting 1¼in (4cm) above the bottom edge of the bottom WW square. The top point on each leaf should be placed ¾in (2cm) in from the outer edges. Pin or glue the leaves temporarily in place, then appliqué to the WW background by hand or machine – we secured ours with top-stitching (**Fig. C**). Finally, join the flowerhead unit to the top WW square to complete the block.

B

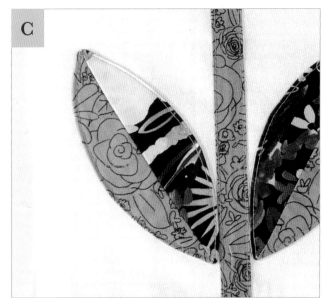

C

Week 25
BIRD 3

UNFINISHED SIZE
6½in (16.5cm) square

TECHNIQUE
Foundation Paper Piecing (FPP)
(see page 49)

WHAT YOU NEED
▸ Templates (see page 172)

▸ **Outer strips:** one 6½ x 1½in (16.5 x 4cm) strip in WW and one 5½ x 1½in (14 x 4cm) strip in WW

▸ **Position A1:** one 4¼in (11.5cm) square in WW – cut in half across the diagonal and discard one triangle

▸ **A2:** one 5½ x 3¼in (14 x 8.5cm) strip in Fab A

▸ **A3:** one 2¼in (6cm) square in Fab D – cut in half across the diagonal and discard one triangle

▸ **A4:** one 4¼ x 1¾in (11 x 4.5cm) strip in Fab D

▸ **A5:** one 2¼in (6cm) square in WW – cut in half across the diagonal and discard one triangle

▸ **B1:** one 2½ x 2¼in (6.5 x 6cm) strip in WW

▸ **B2 & B4:** two 2¼ x 1in (6 x 2.5cm) strips in Fab G

▸ **B3:** one 2¼ x 1¼in (6 x 3.5cm) strip in WW

▸ **B5:** one 2¾ x 2¼in (7 x 6cm) strip in WW

▸ **C1:** one 4¼ x 1¾in (11 x 4.5cm) strip in WW

▸ **C2:** one 2 x 1in (5 x 2.5cm) strip in Fab H

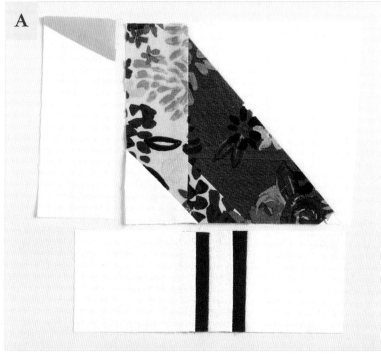

1. Using the templates and following the FPP instructions on page 49, make up the three separate units (**Fig. A**).

2. Arrange the three units in the layout seen in the photograph of the finished block opposite, then stitch them together. There are no rules as to whether you remove the papers before or after stitching the units; it's whatever you prefer! To complete the block, sew the 5½ x 1½in (14 x 4cm) WW strip to the left side, followed by the 6½ x 1½in (16.5 x 4cm) WW strip along the top.

Bottom-right area of the quilt.

SMALL FLOWER 4

UNFINISHED SIZE

6½in (16.5cm) square

TECHNIQUES

Raw Edge Appliqué
(see page 38)

Four-in-One Flying Geese
(see page 27)

WHAT YOU NEED

▶ Fabric adhesive sheets

▶ Template (see page 171)

▶ Four 2⅝in (7cm) squares in WW

▶ One 4½in (11.5cm) square in Fab A

▶ One 3½in (9cm) square in Fab A

▶ Four 2in (5cm) squares in Fab A

▶ One 3in (8cm) square in Fab B

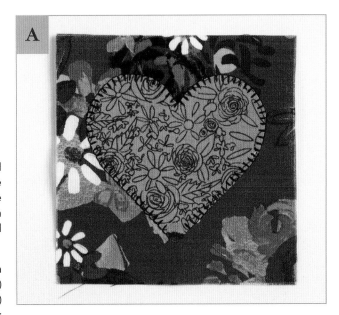

A

I. Using the template provided and Fab B square, and following Steps 1 and 2 of the Raw Edge Appliqué technique on page 38, prepare the heart-shaped appliqué. Centre the heart over the 4½in (11.5cm) Fab A square, iron it in place then appliqué around the edge by machine or hand – we stitched blanket stitch all around by machine (**Fig. A**).

2. Following the Four-in-One Flying Geese technique on page 27, make four Flying Geese units with the 3½in (9cm) Fab A square and 2⅝in (7cm) WW squares. Join a 2in (5cm) square to the right side of one Flying Geese unit (**Fig. B**); repeat with the remaining units.

3. To assemble this block, we'll be sewing a partial seam to start. With RS facing, match the top edge of the centre heart unit to the bottom-right corner of a unit made in Step 2; the left side of the Flying Geese unit will stick out to the left of the centre heart unit (**Fig. C**). Starting in the middle of the centre heart unit, stitch the seam towards the right-hand corner only. Press the Step 2 unit and remaining seams away from the centre heart.

4. Add a second Step 2 unit to the right-hand side of this centre unit, this time stitching along the full length of the centre unit and to the very end of the Step 2 unit. Add the remaining two Step 2 units in the same way. To finish the block, complete the stitching on the partial seam we left unsewn.

B

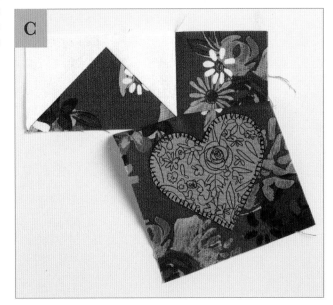

C

CURVED PIECING 1

UNFINISHED SIZE
12½in (32cm) square

TECHNIQUES
Curved Piecing
(see page 36)

Checkerboard – Four Patch
(see page 29)

Appliqué with Card
(see page 40)

WHAT YOU NEED
▶ Paper and thin card
▶ Templates (see page 171)
▶ Twelve 3½in (9cm) squares in WW
▶ One 6½in (16.5cm) square in Fab D
▶ Eight 3½in (9cm) squares in Fab D
▶ Two 3½in (9cm) squares in Fab E
▶ Two 3½in (9cm) squares in Fab F

1. Transfer Templates A and B on to paper, and Template C onto card. Start by making up the centre square. Following the technique on page 29, create a four-patch checkerboard with the 3½in (9cm) Fab E and Fab F squares. Using Template C and following the technique on page 40, create a 5½in (14cm) fabric circle with the four-patch checkerboard and appliqué it onto the 6½in Fab D square by hand or machine – we top-stitched around the edge (**Fig. A**).

2. Cut eight Template A shapes from the eight 3½in (9cm) Fab D squares and eight Template B shapes from eight 3½in (9cm) WW squares. Following the technique on page 36, join an A piece to a B piece to create one unit (**Fig. B**). Repeat to make eight identical units in total.

3. Assemble the units in three rows as shown:

Rows 1 and 3: join two Step 2 units, with the curved edges meeting, then press the seams open. Add a 3½in (9cm) WW square on either side (see the top row of **Fig. C**).

Row 2: stitch two Step 2 units together, again with the curved edges meeting; repeat to make another joined pair. Stitch each pair to either side of the centre unit (see the bottom row of **Fig. C**).

4. Rotate Row 3, so the white 'borders' around the Fab D quarter circles point downwards. Assemble the rows in the layout seen in the photograph of the finished block, opposite, then sew the rows together to complete the block.

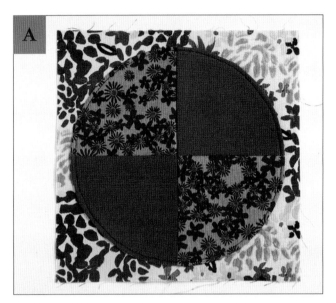

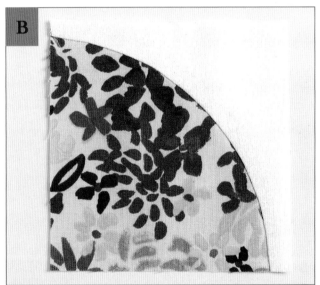

HEART 6

UNFINISHED SIZE
6½in (16.5cm) square

TECHNIQUES
Crazy Patchwork
(see page 28)

Single Flying Geese
(see page 26)

WHAT YOU NEED
▸ Two 3½in (9cm) squares in WW

▸ Four 2in (5cm) squares in WW

▸ Two 3½ x 2in (9 x 5in) strips in Fab D

▸ Scraps of all fabrics used so far to create a piece of crazy patchwork

I. Following the technique on page 28, create a unique Crazy Patchwork unit measuring at least 6½ (16.5cm) wide x 5in (15cm) tall (**Fig. A**). It doesn't have to be exactly that size; you can just trim to size if you end up with a shape that's larger.

2. Draw a diagonal line on the WS of both 3½in (9cm) WW squares. Position one square over the bottom-right corner of the Crazy Patchwork unit, with RS facing and the diagonal line running from top right to bottom left. Stitch along the diagonal line, trim the seam allowance to ¼in (5mm) then press the seam away from the Crazy Patchwork unit. Repeat with the second 3½in (9cm) WW square in the bottom-left corner of the Crazy Patchwork unit, with the diagonal line running from top left to bottom right (**Fig. B**).

3. Following the technique on page 26, create two Flying Geese units with the 3½ x 2in (9 x 5cm) Fab D strips and the 2in (5cm) WW squares. Join these units together along the shortest edges, and with the WW triangles along the top (**Fig. C**); they will form the top of the heart.

4. Stitch the joined Flying Geese units to the top of the Crazy Patchwork unit to complete the block.

Week 29
BASKET 1

UNFINISHED SIZE
12½in (32cm) square

TECHNIQUE
Broderie Perse
(see page 43)

WHAT YOU NEED

- One 7¼in (18.5cm) square in WW – cut in half across the diagonal and discard one piece
- One 7in (18cm) square in WW – cut in half across the diagonal
- One 5⅛in (13cm) square in WW – cut in half across the diagonal
- One 5⅛in (13cm) square in Fab D – cut in half across the diagonal
- One 8½ x 1½in (22 x 4cm) strip in Fab D
- One 9½ x 1½in (24.5 x 4cm) strip in Fab F
- One 6¾in (17.5cm) square in Fab F – cut in half across the diagonal
- Fabric or scraps for Broderie Perse

I. Start with the basket base. Stitch the two 6¾in (17.5cm) Fab F triangles together at right angles. Next, stitch together a 5⅛in (13cm) WW triangle and a 5⅛in (13cm) Fab D triangle at right angles, with the Fab D triangle on the right. Repeat to make a second unit, this time with the Fab D triangle on the left. Join these three units together to form the basket base, centring the seam line on each WW/Fab D unit along the diagonal edges of the Fab F unit. Trim the whole unit to 12½ x 6½in (32 x 16.5cm), if necessary (**Fig. A**).

2. To create the basket top, stitch the 8½ x 1½in (22 x 4cm) Fab D strip to the left side of the 7¼in (18.5cm) WW triangle (with the point of the triangle at the top) then add the 9½ x 1½in (24.5 x 4cm) Fab F strip to the right side. Next, add the two 7in (18cm) WW triangles to the remaining sides of both strips. Trim the whole unit to 12½ x 6½in (32 x 16.5cm) if necessary (**Fig. B**).

3. Join the two units made in Steps 1 and 2, with the Step 2 unit at the top. Following the technique on page 43, cut elements from your fabrics to create a unique Broderie Perse design and appliqué this to your block to finish.

B

Top-right section of the quilt.

Week 30
FLYING GEESE 2

UNFINISHED SIZE
18½ x 6½in (47 x 16.5cm)

TECHNIQUE
Curved Flying Geese

WHAT YOU NEED
▶ Twelve 3½in (9cm) squares in Fab B
▶ Six 3½ x 6½in (9 x 16.5cm) strips in Fab E

I. Fold one Fab E strip in half, WS together, and finger-press. Sandwich this piece between two 3½in (9cm) Fab B squares, RS facing and matching the right-hand and lower edges on all fabrics. The fold of the Fab E piece should be positioned along the top, approx. ¼in (5mm) down from the top edges of the Fab B pieces. Stitch through all the layers along the right-hand edge only (**Fig. A**).

2. Open up the 'sandwich'. From the WS, press the seam open (you'll have three 'squares' on one side of the seam allowance, and one 'square' on the other). On the RS of the joined pieces, pinch the loose corner of the fold of Fab E and pull it down to match the bottom edges of the unit – this will fan out Fab E and create a triangle (**Fig. B**). Press along the diagonal edges of the newly made Fab E triangle. The lower edges of the triangle will be loose, so we recommend machine basting/tacking this edge in place, approx. ⅛in (3mm) within the seam allowance.

3. To create the curves, turn back the two folded edges on the Fab E fabric (these are on the bias and will curve easily). Pin these in place, or run a glue pen along these edges to temporarily secure them, before stitching down the curves either by hand or machine. If you machine stitch, start at the lower edge and sew to just below the point, stop, pivot and sew one stitch across catching both folded back edges, pivot again, then top-stitch back down to finish.

4. To complete the block, join all six units together in a column, with all points facing in the same direction.

Top-right section of the quilt.

Week 31
STAR 6

UNFINISHED SIZE
6½in (16.5cm) square

TECHNIQUES
Two-in-One Half Square Triangles
(see page 19)

Quarter Square Triangles
(see page 23)

WHAT YOU NEED
▶ Two 3½in (9cm) squares in WW
▶ Two 3in (8cm) squares in WW
▶ One 2½in (6.5cm) square in WW
▶ Two 3½in (9cm) squares in Fab G
▶ Two 3in (8cm) squares in Fab G
▶ One 2½in (6.5cm) square in Fab G

A

I. Create four Half Square Triangle units with 3in (8cm) Fab G and WW squares, and four Quarter Square Triangle units with the 3½in (9cm) Fab G and WW squares (**Fig. A**). Trim all units to 2½in (6.5cm) square if necessary. Discard one of the Half Square Triangles.

2. Assemble the units in three columns as follows, working from the top downwards (see **Fig. B**):

Column 1: Half Square Triangle (Fab G triangle on top), Quarter Square Triangle (Fab G triangles top and bottom), 2½in (6.5cm) WW square.

Column 2: Quarter Square Triangle (Fab G triangles top and bottom), Half Square Triangle (WW triangle on top), Quarter Square Triangle (WW triangles top and bottom).

Column 3: 2½in (6.5cm) Fab G square, Quarter Square Triangle (WW triangles top and bottom), Half Square Triangle (Fab G triangle on top).

3. Join the three columns together to complete the block.

B

Week 32
STAR 7

UNFINISHED SIZE
6½in (16.5cm) square

TECHNIQUE
Foundation Paper Piecing (FPP)
(see page 49)

WHAT YOU NEED
▶ Paper
▶ Template (page 172)
▶ Four 2½in (6.5cm) squares in WW
▶ Eight 2¼ x 1¾in (6 x 4.5cm) strips in WW
▶ Two 1¾in (3.5cm) squares in Fab C – cut each in half across both diagonals to make eight triangles
▶ One 2½in (6.5cm) square in Fab C
▶ Four 2¾ x 1¾in (7 x 4.5cm) strips in Fab F

1. Make four copies of the FPP template. Following the technique on page 49 and with one copy of the template, assemble one unit in the following order: Fab F strip over position 1, 2¼ x 1¾in (6 x 4.5cm) WW strips over positions 2 and 3, Fab C triangle over positions 4 and 5. Construct three more identical units to make four units in total. Trim around the outer edges, allowing for a ¼in (5mm) seam allowance (**Fig. A**). If you wish, remove the papers now before assembling the rows.

2. Assemble the block in three rows as follows:

Rows 1 and 3: Stitch a 2½in (6.5cm) WW square either side of one FPP unit (see the top row of **Fig. B**).

Row 2: Stitch a FPP unit either side of the 2½in (6.5cm) Fab C square (see the bottom row of **Fig. B**).

3. Arrange the rows as seen in the photograph of the finished block above, rotating Row 3 so the Fab F triangle points downwards. Stitch the rows together to complete the block.

A

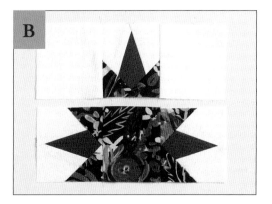

B

Week 33
LOG CABIN 2

UNFINISHED SIZE
12½in (32cm) square

TECHNIQUE
Log Cabin
(see page 30)

WHAT YOU NEED

Using two different widths of strips in this version of log cabin gives the block the illusion of it being curved. Since there are lots of pieces in this block, we've listed them below in the order they are used.

▸ **1:** Four 1½in (4cm) squares in Fab G

▸ **2:** Four 1½ x 1in (4 x 2.5cm) strips in WW

▸ **3:** Four 2 x 1in (5 x 2.5cm) strips WW

▸ **4:** Four 2 x 1½in (5 x 4cm) strips in Fab E

▸ **5:** Four 3 x 1½in (8 x 4cm) strips in Fab B

▸ **6:** Four 3 x 1in (8 x 2.5cm) strips in WW

▸ **7:** Four 3½ x 1in (9 x 2.5cm) strips in WW

▸ **8:** Four 3½ x 1½in (9 x 4cm) strips in Fab D

▸ **9:** Four 4½ x 1½in (11.5 x 4cm) strips in Fab F

▸ **10:** Four 4½ x 1in (11.5 x 2.5cm) strips in WW

▸ **11:** Four 5 x 1in (13 x 2.5cm) strips in WW

▸ **12:** Four 5 x 1½in (13 x 4cm) strips in Fab C

▸ **13:** Four 6 x 1½in (15.5 x 4cm) strips in Fab A

▸ **14:** Two 11½ x 1in (29.5 x 2.5cm) strips and two 12½ x 1in (32 x 2.5cm) strips in WW for the outer edges

I. Refer to the technique on page 30 throughout as you assemble your block. Note you will work in a counterclockwise direction. Stitch one no. 1 Fab G square and one no. 2 WW strip together then press the seams towards the WW piece. Rotate the unit so the WW strip is on top, then add the next WW strip (no. 3) to the left side of the centre unit. Add the Fab E strip (no. 4) to the lower edge. Continue adding strips in the numbered order, working your way around the centre, until you finish with the 6 x 1½in (15.5cm) Fab A strip (no. 13) – see **Fig. A**. Make three more identical units.

2. Arrange the units in the layout seen in the photograph of the finished block above, rotating units where necessary. Join the units in pairs together first, then join the pairs together as shown. Add the 11½ x 1in (29.5 x 2.5cm) WW strips to the side edges, followed by the 12½ x 1in (32.2.5cm) strips to the top and bottom edges to complete the block.

A

Week 34
HEART 7

UNFINISHED SIZE
6½in (16.5cm) square

TECHNIQUES
Raw Edge Appliqué
(see page 38)

Checkerboard – Four Patch
(see page 29)

WHAT YOU NEED
▶ Fabric adhesive sheets
▶ Templates (see page 170)
▶ Four 2¾in (7cm) squares in WW
▶ Two 3½in (9cm) squares in Fab B
▶ Two 2¼in (6cm) squares in Fab B
▶ Two 3½in (9cm) squares in Fab E
▶ Two 2¼in (6cm) squares in Fab E

1. Using the templates provided and a Fab B square, and following Steps 1 and 2 of the Raw Edge Appliqué technique on page 38, prepare the heart appliqué shapes – you need four large WW hearts and two small hearts in both Fab B and Fab E.

2. Take one of the 3½in (9cm) coloured squares and machine appliqué the larger WW heart in the centre of it (we used zigzag stitch). Next, stitch one of the small coloured hearts on top of the WW heart, matching the points at the lower edge and ensuring it's in an alternate colourway to the background square (**Fig. A**). Repeat the process to make four units, two in each colourway.

3. Arrange the units in the layout seen in the photograph of the finished block above. Follow the Four-Patch Checkerboard technique on page 29 to assemble the block.

A

LARGE PIECED BLOCK 2

UNFINISHED SIZE
12½in (32cm) square

TECHNIQUES
Four-in-One Half Square Triangles
(see page 20)

Eight-in-One Half Square Triangles
(see page 21)

WHAT YOU NEED
▶ Two 6¼in (16cm) squares in WW
▶ One 4¼in (11cm) square in WW
▶ Two 6¼in (16cm) squares in Fab C
▶ One 4¼in (11cm) square in Fab C
▶ Eight 2½in (6.5cm) squares in Fab C
▶ Two 4¼in (11cm) squares Fab G
▶ Four 2½in (6.5cm) squares in Fab G

TIPS

– For this block, you may find it helps to press some of the bulky seams open.

– As there are many seams within the block, we suggest you stitch with a scant ¼in (5mm) seam allowance.

– Once you have patched the corner, side and centre units, the block will come together like a nine patch.

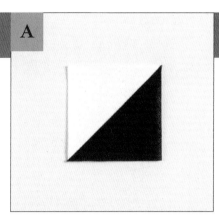

A

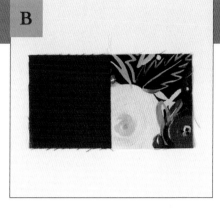

B

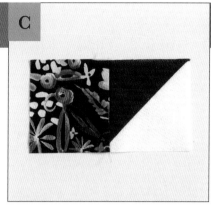

C

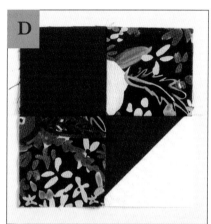

D

E

F

I. Following the Four-in-One Half Square Triangle technique on page 20, create the four Half Square Triangles with one 4¼in (11cm) Fab G square and one 4¼in (11cm) WW square. Press and trim to 2½in (6.5cm) square (**Fig. A**). Repeat to make four units in total.

2. Next, stitch a 2½in (6.5cm) Fab C and Fab G square together (**Fig. B**). Repeat to make four units in total.

3. Stitch a 2½in (6.5cm) Fab C square to the left of a Half Square Triangle unit made in Step 1 (**Fig. C**). Repeat to make four identical units in total.

4. Sew one unit made in Step 2 to the top of a unit made in Step 3 (**Fig. D**). Repeat to make four corner units in total.

5. Following the Eight-in-One Half Square Triangle technique on page 21, make up sixteen Half Square Triangle units using the 6¼in (16cm) Fab C and WW squares. Press and trim each to 2½in (6.5cm) square. Assemble four of your Half Square Triangles as shown in **Fig. E**, stitching them together in pairs first then stitching the pairs together. Repeat to make four identical chevron-design units in total.

6. Following the Four-in-One Half Square Triangle technique on page 20, make up four Half Square Triangles with the 4¼in (11cm) Fab C and G squares. Press and trim each to 2½in (6.5cm) square. Lay out the 4 units as shown in **Fig. F** then stitch them together to make the centre unit.

7. Arrange the nine units in the layout seen in the photograph of the finished block opposite. Start by stitching the three units in each row together first, then stitch the three rows together to complete the block.

Week 36

FLYING GEESE 3

UNFINISHED SIZE
18½ x 6½in (47 x 16.5cm)

TECHNIQUE
Foundation Paper Piecing (FPP)
(see page 49)

WHAT YOU NEED
▸ Paper
▸ Template (page 173)
▸ Six 4½in (11.5cm) squares in WW –
  cut each across the diagonal to
  create twelve pieces
▸ Three 4½in (11.5cm) squares in
  Fab C – each cut each across the
  diagonal to create six pieces
▸ Six 1¼ x 4½in (3.5 x 11.5cm) strips
  in Fab H
▸ Six 1¼ x 5¼in (3.5 x 13.5cm) strips
  in Fab H

I. Make six copies of the template. Following the technique on page 49 and with one copy of the template, assemble one unit in the following order: one Fab C triangle over position 1, shorter Fab H strip over position 2, longer Fab H strip over position 3, WW triangles over positions 4 and 5. Construct five more identical units.

2. Join the six units with all the points running in the same direction, stitching them together in pairs first, then stitch the pairs together to complete the block.

Week 37
BIRD 4

UNFINISHED SIZE
6½in (16.5cm) square

TECHNIQUE
Raw Edge Appliqué
(see page 38)

WHAT YOU NEED
▸ Fabric adhesive sheets
▸ Templates (see page 173)
▸ One 6½in (16.5cm) square in WW
▸ One 4½ x 2¾in (11.5 x 7cm) strip in Fab A
▸ One 4¼ x 2¾in (11 x 7cm) strip in Fab F
▸ One 6½in x 2¼in (16.5 x 6cm) strip in Fab G
▸ Fabric scraps in Fab B, E & H

1. Trace the templates onto fabric adhesive sheets. Following Steps 1 and 2 of the technique on page 38, prepare your appliqué shapes – branch (Fab G), bird body (Fab A), bird wings (Fab F) and bird tails (Fab B, E and H scraps).

2. To build up the picture in this block, start with the branch. Position the top of the branch over the 6½in (16.5cm) WW square, 3in (8cm) down on the right-hand side and 4½in (11.5cm) down on the left. Stitch in place (we used zigzag stitch).

3. Next, position the bird body sitting on the top of the branch, with the head approx. ¾in (2cm) from the top of the block and 1in (2.5cm) from the right; the left side of the body should be approx. 2¼in (6cm) in from the left. At this stage press only the head in position.

4. Tuck the tail feathers under the lower edge of the bird by approx. ⅛in (3mm), overlapping them slightly. Tuck the larger wing under the curve of the bird's back, with the top of the wing approx. ¾in (2cm) from the top of the block. Press these pieces into position then stitch over the visible edges with the same stitch used before. Press then stitch down the bird. Lastly, position the smaller wing on top of the bird, as shown, 2in (5cm) down from the top of the block, approx. 1⅞in (5cm) from the right and with the wing tip 3¼in (8.5cm) down from the top.

HEART 8

UNFINISHED SIZE

6½in (16.5cm) square

TECHNIQUES

Checkerboard – Four Patch
(see page 29)

Reverse Appliqué
(see page 44)

Raw Edge Appliqué (optional)
(see page 38)

WHAT YOU NEED

▸ Template (see page 174)

▸ One 6½in (16.5cm) square of
freezer paper

▸ One 5½in (14cm) square in WW

▸ Two 2¾in (7cm) squares in Fab C

▸ Two 2¾in (7cm) squares in Fab D

▸ One 1 x 5½in (2.5 x 14cm) strip in Fab D

▸ One 1 x 6in (2.5 x 15.5cm) strip in Fab C

▸ One 1 x 6in (2.5 x 15.5cm) strip in Fab D

▸ One 1 x 6½in (2.5 x 16.5cm) strip in Fab C

A

1. Following the technique on page 29, create a four-patch unit with the 2¾in (7cm) Fab C and Fab D squares (**Fig. A**). Set this aside.

2. Starting from the top, add the 1in (2.5cm) Fab D and Fab C border strips around the 5½in (14cm) WW square, in a clockwise direction and in the following order: 1 x 5½in (2.5 x 14cm) in Fab D, 1 x 6in (2.5 x 15.5cm) in Fab C, 1 x 6in (2.5 x 15.5cm) in Fab D, 1 x 6½in (2.5 x 16.5cm) in Fab C. With the templates provided, and referring to the technique on page 44, prepare this background square for reverse appliqué.

3. After removing the freezer paper, and with the RS facing uppermost, position the four-patch unit under the cut-out heart shape, matching the centre seamline with the points on the heart. Secure the layers with your glue pen, pins or basting/tacking stitches. Hand or machine appliqué around the heart (we used slip stitch). If you prefer to use raw edge appliqué, follow the instructions for Step 3 on page 38. Trim off any excess checkerboard fabric from the reverse of the block, leaving a ¼in (5mm) seam allowance all around.

Close-up of the Tall Flower 3 block on the finished quilt (see page 116 for instructions on making the block).

TALL FLOWER 3

UNFINISHED SIZE
18½ x 6½in (47 x 16.5cm)

TECHNIQUE
Machine Piecing

WHAT YOU NEED
▸ Twelve 2¾ x 1⅜in (7 x 3.5cm) strips in WW
▸ Twenty-four 1in (2.5cm) squares in WW
▸ Two 3½in (9cm) squares in Fab A
▸ Six 3½ x 1¼in (9 x 3.5cm) strips in Fab B
▸ Six 2½ x 1¾in (6.5 x 4.5cm) strips in Fab B
▸ Twelve 1in (2.5cm) squares in Fab B
▸ Two 3½in (9cm) squares in Fab C
▸ Two 3½in (9cm) squares in Fab D

1. Draw a diagonal line across the WS of all the 1in (2.5cm) WW and Fab B squares.

2. Make a flowerhead unit: first position a 1in (2.5cm) WW square over the top right-hand corner of the 3½in (9cm) Fab A square, RS facing and with the diagonal running from top left to bottom right. Stitch along the diagonal line, trim the seam allowance to ¼in (5mm) then press. Repeat the process to add a second WW square in the bottom right-hand corner (diagonal running from top right to bottom left), a 1in (2.5cm) Fab B square in the bottom-left corner (diagonal running from top left to bottom right), and a second Fab B square in the top-left corner (diagonal running from top right to bottom left) (**Fig. A**).

3. Repeat Step 2 to make a second identical flowerhead unit with the 3½in (9cm) Fab A square as the background, two flowerhead units using the 3½in (9cm) Fab C square as a backgrounds, and two flowerhead units using the 3½in (9cm) Fab D squares as the backgrounds. Six flowerhead units in total.

4. Make a leaf unit: stitch a 1in (2.5cm) WW square to the top right and bottom left corners of the 2½ x 1¾in (6.5 x 4.5cm) Fab B strip, in the same way described in Step 2. Add a 2¾ x 1⅜in (7 x 3.5cm) WW strip above and below this unit, then stitch a 3½ x 1¼in (9 x 3.5cm) Fab B strip to the right-hand side to complete the unit (**Fig. B**). Make six identical units in total.

5. Stitch a flowerhead unit to the 'stem' side of each leaf unit, ensuring that the Fab B triangles of each flowerhead unit are along the joining edge.

6. Assemble the block, referring to the photograph of the finished block opposite if needed: starting at the top and inverting alternate flowerhead units, stitch the units together in the following flowerhead order: Fab A, Fab D, Fab C, Fab A, Fab D and Fab C.

BASKET 2

UNFINISHED SIZE
12½in (32cm) square

TECHNIQUE
Bias & Straight Strips
(see page 45)

WHAT YOU NEED
▸ One 12½ x 2½in (32 x 6.5cm) strip in WW
▸ Two 2½in (6.5cm) squares in WW
▸ Eighteen 1½in (4cm) squares in WW
▸ Four 2½in (6.5cm) squares in Fab A
▸ One 14 x 1in (35.5 x 2.5cm) strip in Fab B
▸ Six 2½in (6.5cm) squares in Fab B
▸ Four 2½in (6.5cm) squares in Fab C
▸ Four 2½in (6.5cm) squares in Fab E
▸ One 12½ x 4½in (32 x 11.5cm) strip in Fab H

1. Create the flowerhead unit: first, draw a diagonal line across the WS of each 1½in (4cm) WW square. With RS facing, position the WW square over the top right-hand corner of a 2½in (6.5cm) Fab A square, with the diagonal running from top left to bottom right. Stitch along the diagonal line, trim the seam allowance to ¼in (5mm) and press. Repeat to make four identical units in total.

2. Referring to the layout seen in **Fig. A**, rotate then stitch the Step 1 units together in a pinwheel-like design (pay particular attention to the positioning of the white triangles) – first in pairs then join the pairs to create a four-patch unit.

3. Repeat Steps 1 and 2 with the 2½in (6.5cm) Fab C and Fab E squares. Join the three flower units together to complete Row 1 (**Fig. A**).

4. Create the leaves and stems unit: repeat the instructions in Step 1 with the six 2½in (6.5cm) Fab B squares and six 1½in (4cm) WW squares, this time with three WW triangles in the top-left corners and three WW triangles in the top-right corners. Stitch the Fab 2 units together in pairs with the WW triangles meeting at the centre top. Stitch the pairs together, in a row. Add the 12½ x 2½in (32 x 6.5cm) WW strip to the top of this unit. Following the technique on page 45, create a single long stem piece with the 14in (35.5cm) Fab B strip. Cut the stem into three 4½in (11.5cm) lengths. Position each stem vertically between the WW triangles then top-stitch in place. This completes Row 2 of the block (**Fig. B**).

5. Create the basket: draw diagonal lines across the WS of the 2½in (6.5cm) WW squares. Add these to the bottom corners the Fab H strip in the same way described in Step 1, with the diagonal of the bottom-right WW square running from top right to bottom left, and the diagonal of the bottom-left WW square running from top left to bottom right. This completes Row 3 of the block (**Fig. C**).

6. To complete the block, join the three rows together.

A

B

C

DRESDEN 2

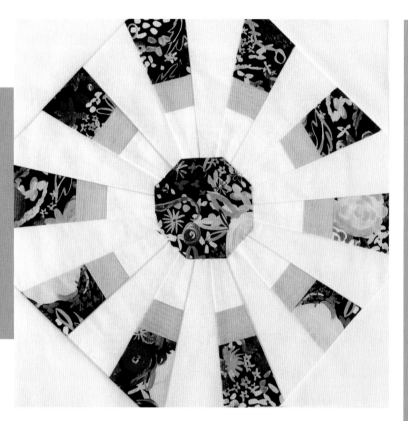

UNFINISHED SIZE
12½in (32cm) square

TECHNIQUES
Dresden Plate
(see page 32)

Needleturn Appliqué
(see page 39)

WHAT YOU NEED
▸ Templates (see page 175)

▸ One 30 x 2¼in (76.5 x 6cm) strip in WW

▸ One 20 x 5½in (51 x 14cm) strip in WW

▸ Two 5in (13cm) squares in WW –
  cut each in half across the diagonal to
  make four pieces

▸ One 30 x 2¾in (76.5 x 7cm) strip in Fab C

▸ One 3¾in (9.5cm) square in Fab C

▸ One 30 x 1½in (76.5 x 4cm) strip in Fab H

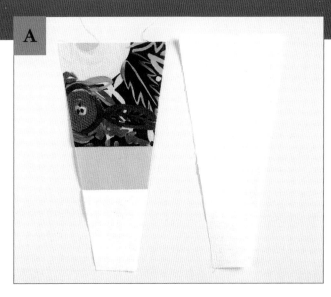

A

1. Start by stitching the 30 x 2¾in (76.5 x 7cm) Fab C strip and the 30 x 1½in (76.5 x 4cm) Fab H strip together, then sew the 30 x 2¼in (76.5 x 6cm) WW strip to the opposite edge of Fab H. Press the seams then rotate the unit so Fab C is at the top. Using the wedge template provided, and with the widest section at the top, cut 10 wedge shapes from the unit. Also cut 10 wedge shapes from the 20 x 5½in (51 x 14cm) WW strip (**Fig. A**). (Note: if your WW fabric is non-directional, these can be topped and tailed to save fabric.)

2. Join the 20 wedges to create a circle with a circular hole in the middle, alternating the Fab C/Fab H/WW and WW colourways. To cut the circle into an octagon, fold the whole unit in half then in half once more, then open out the unit again; you should have four points creased. Mark or crease between each fold (these final marks will be on a seam line). Between each mark, cut off the excess fabric along the outside edges – the measurement between opposite edges should be 12½in (32cm) across (**Fig. B**).

3. To make the appliqué centre, use the octagon template to cut an octagon from the 3¾in (9.5cm) Fab C square, adding a ¼in (5mm) seam allowance all around. Turn under each side of the octagon fabric by ¼in (5mm) and press (**Fig. C**).

4. To complete the block, stitch the WW triangles to the four corners of the wedge unit, matching up the centre points on the diagonals of the triangles with the diagonal outer sides of the wedge unit. Appliqué the octagon shape over the centre hole – we used slip stitch. Finally, trim the whole block to a 12½in (32cm) square.

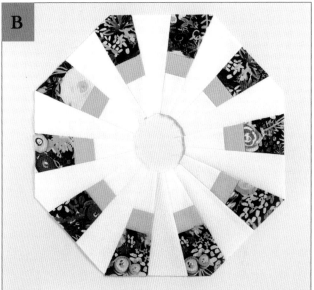

B

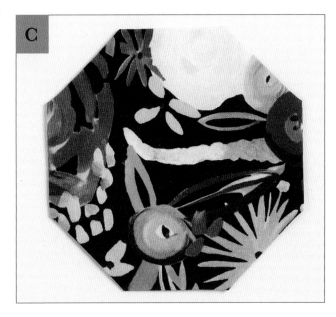

C

Week 42
STAR 8

UNFINISHED SIZE
6½in (16.5cm) square

TECHNIQUES
Single Half Square Triangle
(see page 19)

Split Half Square Triangles
(see page 22)

Square within a Square – Method 2
(see page 34)

WHAT YOU NEED
▸ Four 2⅝in (7cm) squares in WW –
cut each across the diagonal and
discard one piece
▸ Four 2½in (6.5cm) squares in WW
▸ Two 2⅝in (7cm) squares in Fab A
▸ One 1⅞in (5cm) square in Fab A –
cut in half across the diagonal and
discard one piece
▸ One 2in (5cm) square in Fab B
▸ One 1⅞in (5cm) square in Fab C –
cut in half across the diagonal and
discard one piece
▸ Two 2⅝in (7cm) squares in Fab C
▸ One 1⅞in (5cm) square in D –
cut in half across the diagonal and
discard one piece
▸ Two 2⅝in (7cm) squares in Fab D
▸ One 1⅞in (5cm) squares in Fab E –
cut in half across the diagonal and
discard one piece
▸ Two 2⅝in (7cm) squares in Fab E

1. Following the technique on page 34, create a Square within a Square unit with points using the 2in (5cm) Fab B square and the four 1⅞in (5cm) triangles in Fab A, C, D and E. Start by attaching the Fab E triangle (top right) then the Fab C triangle (bottom left), followed by Fab D (top left) and lastly Fab A (bottom right). Trim to 2½in (6.5cm) square (**Fig. A**). This forms the central unit of the block.

2. Following the technique on page 19, create four single Half Square Triangle units with the 2⅝in (7cm) WW squares and one 2⅝in (7cm) square each in Fab A, C, D and E. Following the technique on page 22, add the contrasting third colour to the Half Square Triangle units as follows: 2⅝in (7cm) Fab E square on Fab D/WW (unit 1), 2⅝in (7cm) Fab D square on Fab C/WW (unit 2), 2⅝in (7cm) Fab A square on Fab E/WW (unit 3), and 2⅝in (7cm) Fab C square on Fab A/WW (unit 4). Trim each unit to 2½in (6.5cm) square (**Fig. B**).

3. Assemble the rows as follows:

Row 1: stitch a 2½in (6.5cm) WW square either side of unit 1.

Row 2: stitch unit 2 to the left and unit 3 to the right of the centre unit.

Row 3: stitch a 2½in (6.5cm) WW square either side of unit 4.

4. Join the three rows together to complete the block.

A

B

Week 43
SMALL FLOWER 5

I. Using the template and the technique on page 41 or the technique on page 42, prepare and create eight Fab C petals, adding a scant ¼in (5mm) seam allowance all around. The petals are all the same shape, but you'll need to extend the length of each so they fit under the centre.

2. Referring to the placement diagram on page 174, stitch the petals into position on the 6½in (16.5cm) WW square by hand or machine, ensuring that the three petals on the left hand side and bottom edge are stitched right into the seam allowance and extend beyond the edges of the block (**Fig. A**). Cut off the excess fabric from these petals when the block is complete. Don't worry about turning under the flat ends of the petals where they'll be tucked under the circle.

3. Make the Fab E centre circle following the technique on page 40. Position this over the centre of the flower then stitch in place to complete the block.

UNFINISHED SIZE
6½in (16.5cm) square

TECHNIQUES
Appliqué with Card
(see page 40)

Appliqué with Freezer Paper
(see page 41)

Appliqué with Interfacing
(see page 42)

Needleturn Appliqué
(see page 39)

WHAT YOU NEED
▸ Templates and placement diagram
(see page 174)
▸ Freezer paper or interfacing
▸ One 6½in (16.5cm) square in WW
▸ One 18 x 3½in (46 x 9cm) strip in Fab C
▸ One 2½in (6.5cm) square in Fab E

TIP
We appliquéd this block by hand with needleturn appliqué, but you could use the other methods if you wish.

You could also use the Raw Edge Appliqué technique (see page 38) if you like this style.

A

Week 44

BIRD 5

UNFINISHED SIZE
6½in (16.5cm) square

TECHNIQUES
Raw Edge Appliqué
(see page 38)

WHAT YOU NEED
▶ Fabric adhesive sheets
▶ Templates (see page 174)
▶ One 6½in (16.5cm) square in WW
▶ One 3½ x 3¼in (9 x 8.5cm) strip in Fab B
▶ One 4 x 3in (10 x 8cm) strip in Fab C
▶ One 4 x 3in (10 x 8cm) strip in Fab D
▶ One 3½ x 3¼in (9 x 8.5cm) strip in Fab E
▶ One 6½ x ½in (16.5 x 1.5cm) strip in Fab G

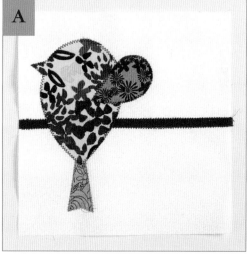

1. Using the templates provided and following the technique on page 38, prepare all the appliqué pieces onto the necessary fabrics with the fabric adhesive sheets – bird bodies (Fab C and Fab D), bird wings (Fab B and Fab E) and bird tails (again, Fab B and Fab E).

2. To build up the picture, start by positioning the branch (6½ x ½in or 16.5 x 1.5cm Fab G strip) across the centre of the 6½in (16.5cm) WW square, and stitch in place. Next position the Fab D bird body approx. ¾in (2cm) down from the top of the block and ⅜in (1cm) from the left. Press the top two-thirds of the body only. Insert the Fab B tail underneath the bottom of the body. Appliqué the visible edge around the tail, then stitch all around the bird body. To complete the first bird, stagger the Fab E wing over the right-hand side of the bird body, 1⅛in (3cm) down from the top of the body and 2¼in (6cm) in from the left of the block (**Fig. A**).

3. With the remaining fabric pieces, make up the second bird in the same way, albeit upside down. If you rotate the block, the placement will be the same as described in Step 1.

Week 45
BASKET 3

UNFINISHED SIZE
12½in (32cm) square

TECHNIQUES
Foundation Paper Piecing (FPP)
(see page 49)

Bias & Straight Strips
(see page 45)

WHAT YOU NEED
As there are several pieces in this block, we've grouped the cutting details into two sections.

BASKET & LOWER BACKGROUND:

▸ One 18 x 1in (46 x 2.5cm) bias strip in Fab A

▸ Four 2⅝in (7cm) squares in Fab A

▸ Two 3in (8cm) squares in Fab B – cut each in half across the diagonal to make four pieces

▸ Two 2⅝in (7cm) squares in Fab B

▸ One 3in (8cm) square in Fab A – cut in half across the diagonal to make two pieces

▸ Two 7¼in x 2⅝in (18.5 x 7cm) strips in WW

▸ One 3⅞in (10cm) WW square – cut in half across the diagonal to make two pieces

FLOWER & UPPER BACKGROUND:

▸ Templates (see page 175)

▸ Paper

▸ Four 2¼ x 1½in (6 x 4cm) strips in WW

▸ Four 2in (5cm) squares in Fab G – cut each in half across the diagonal to make eight pieces

▸ Four 2in (5cm) squares in WW

▸ One 2¼in (6cm) square in Fab G

▸ One 3½ x 3in (9 x 8cm) strip in WW

▸ One 3½ x 1in strip (9 x 2.5cm) in WW

▸ One 6½in (16.5cm) square in WW

▸ One 6½ x 3½in (16.5 x 9cm) strip in WW

A

I. Following the technique on page 45, prepare the 18 x 1in (46 x 2.5cm) Fab A bias strip. Set this aside.

2. For the basket, we advise laying out all the pieces for it before sewing in place, so you can see exactly how they come together. Stitch the 2⅝in (7cm) Fab A and Fab B squares and the 3in (8cm) Fab B triangles together, alternating the colourways as follows:

Section 1 (left side of basket): Stitch a 2⅝in (7cm) Fab A square either side of a 2⅝in (7cm) Fab B square then add a 3in (8cm) Fab B triangle to the top of that unit. (Note: the edges of the Fab B triangles at the top of the basket are on the bias/diagonal).

Section 2: Stitch a 2⅝in (7cm) Fab A square to the left side of a 2⅝in (7cm) Fab B square, then add a 3in (8cm) Fab B triangle to the top of this unit, as before.

Section 3: Stitch a 3in (8cm) Fab B triangle to the top of a 2⅝in (7cm) Fab A square as before, then add the final 3in (8cm) Fab B triangle to the right side of the Fab A square.

Join the three sections together.

3. Next, stitch the 7¼in x 2⅝in (18.5 x 7cm) WW strips to the 3in (8cm) Fab A triangles (again, be aware the bias/diagonal edges of these triangles will form the lower edge). Sew these units to either side of the basket, as shown. Lastly, stitch the 3⅞in (10cm) WW triangles across the lower corners to complete the lower half of the block (**Fig. A**).

Continued > > >

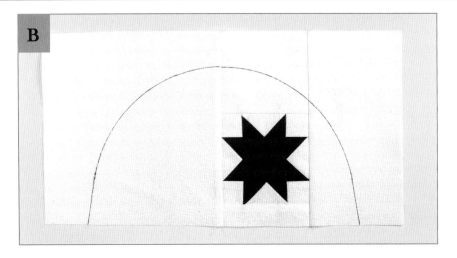

4. Make one copy of the templates. Referring to the placement shown in each section on the templates and following the FPP technique on page 49, make up the four sections of the flower unit (see centre-right unit in **Fig. B**). The following fabrics were used for the different positions:

A1, B1, C1 and D1: 2¼ x 1½in (6 x 4cm) WW strips

A2/A3, B2/B3, C2/C3 and D2/D3: 2in (5cm) Fab G triangles

B4/B5 and C4/C5: 2in (5cm) WW squares

A4: 2¼in (6cm) Fab G square.

5. To make up the top of the block (where the handle and flower unit sit), begin by stitching the D section to the bottom edge of the A section (so it's next to A4). Stitch the B and C sections either side of the A/D unit. Stitch the 3½ x 3in (9 x 8cm) WW strip to the top edge of the flower unit and the 3½ x 1in (9 x 2.5cm) strip to the bottom edge. Next stitch the 6½in (16.5cm) WW square to the left-hand side of the flower unit and the 6½ x 3½in (16.5 x 9cm) WW strip to the right-hand side. Mark the semi-circular position for the underside of the handle (we used a small dinner plate as a template) – approx. 1¼in (3.5cm) down from the centre top and 1½in (4cm) in from each side on the bottom edge. Glue, pin or baste/tack the Fab A bias strip in position then appliqué using your chosen method; we used slip stitch.

6. Stitch the basket and top of the block together to finish.

FLYING GEESE 4

UNFINISHED SIZE
18½ x 12½in (47 x 32cm)

TECHNIQUE
Machine piecing

WHAT YOU NEED
▶ Two 5¼in (13.5cm) squares in WW –
  cut each in half across the diagonal
  to create four pieces
▶ Four 4⅞in (12.5cm) squares in Fab A
▶ One 2⅞in (7.5cm) square in Fab A –
  cut in half across the diagonal then
  discard one piece
▶ Two 1½ x 6½in (4 x 16.5cm) strips in Fab A

TIPS

– The 'geese' are in the WW fabric,
the background is Fab A.

– This is a slightly different way of
making Flying Geese units.

– You will be working with diagonal
edges, so you may wish to starch your
fabric to avoid stretching.

I. With RS facing, position a 5¼in (13.5cm) WW triangle on top of a 4⅞in (12.5cm) Fab A square, with the diagonal running from top left to bottom right. Stitch across the top and down the right side (see the top-left unit in **Fig. A**). Cut the unit in half along the diagonal, from top right to bottom left (see the top-right unit in **Fig. A**). Press the WW triangles away from the Fab A pieces (see the bottom unit in **Fig. A**). Keep the two different directions – left and right – in separate piles. Repeat with the remaining 5¼in (13.5cm) WW triangles and 4⅞in (12.5cm) Fab A squares. To help create sharp points and keep the whole block straight later on, we suggest you mark an 'X' ¼in (5mm) in on the WS of all corners of the units. Unpick one right-hand piece and keep these pieces separate.

2. The block is constructed from the bottom upwards. With the single WW triangle on the right, stitch a left-hand unit on the left (part of that unit will hang below the seam line; this will be trimmed later). Press this seam towards the WW triangle; the other seams will be pressed towards the Fab A triangles (**Fig. B**). Add a right-hand unit to the right of the first WW triangle in the same way (**Fig. C**).

3. Continue adding right- and left-hand units alternately, matching up the previously marked 'X's (it helps to put a pin through both to hold together before stitching).

4. To square up the top, add the 2⅞in (7.5cm) Fab A triangle to the left-hand side and finally the larger, unpicked Fab A triangle to the right. To square off the lower end, cut off the extended point of the Fab A triangle.

5. To complete the block, add a 1½ x 6½in (4 x 16.5cm) Fab A strip to the top and bottom ends. Note that this block will be sewn into the quilt with the 'geese' flying downwards.

A

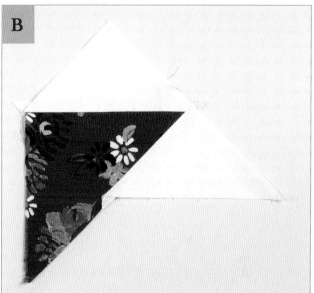

B

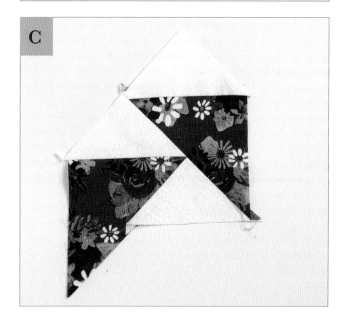

C

ENGLISH PAPER PIECING 2

UNFINISHED SIZE
12½in (32cm) square

TECHNIQUE
English Paper Piecing (EPP)
(see page 46)

WHAT YOU NEED
▸ Paper or thin card
▸ Template (see page 172)
▸ One 12½in (32cm) square in WW
▸ One 17½ x 2½in (44.5 x 6.5cm) strip in Fab D
▸ One 17½ x 2½in (44.5 x 6.5cm) strip in Fab G
▸ One 23 x 2½in (58.5 x 6.5cm) strip in Fab C

TIPS

– Although measurements are given, this is a good block to use up those fabric scraps.

– This design, using the applecore template, comes together in a slightly different way to conventional EPP, so follow the full instructions carefully.

A

B

1. Using the template and following Steps 1 and 2 of the techniques on page 46, reproduce 30 shapes from the following fabrics: 12 shapes in Fab C, nine shapes in Fab D, nine shapes in Fab G (**Fig. A**). At this stage, turn under then glue or baste/tack the fabric to the convex (outward) curved edges only.

2. We'll be stitching six rows of five shapes. For Rows 1, 3 and 5 start with a Fab G shape on its side, and a Fab C shape the right way up. Position the covered convex curve of the Fab G shape over the Fab C seam allowance, butting the two curves together and centring them (holding the shapes up to the light will help with matching these edges accurately). It's important that the top and bottom seam lines on both shapes match as well. Keeping the RS uppermost, glue, pin or baste/tack the shapes in place before sewing them together with slip stitch along the Fab G curve. Repeat to make a second identical pair, then sew these pairs together. Add a third Fab G shape to the end of the joined pairs to complete the row (**Fig. B**). Make three identical rows in total.

Continued > > >

3. Follow the same process in Step 2 to join the shapes for Rows 2, 4 and 6, using the Fab C and D shapes. For these rows, note the Fab D shapes are the right way up and the Fab C shapes are on their side (**Fig. C**).

4. With RS facing, place Row 1 on top of Row 2 and interlock them, matching the seam lines. Hold the rows together by glueing, pinning or basting/tacking within the seam allowance before securing them with slip stitch (**Fig. D**). Repeat to join Rows 3 and 4, then join the row pairs together. Add Row 5 in the same way to complete the block.

5. When the panel is complete, on the outside edges, clip the concave curves, fold back the fabric and press the seam allowance over the papers (a spray of starch will help to hold in place). Gently remove all papers, position your panel diagonally on the 12½in (32cm) WW square, ¾in (2cm) in from each side and 1in (2.5cm) in from the top and bottom edges, and appliqué in place using your chosen method.

TALL FLOWER 4

UNFINISHED SIZE
18½ x 6½in (47 x 16.5cm)

TECHNIQUE
Bias & Straight Strips
(see page 45)

WHAT YOU NEED

▸ One 7¾ x 6½in (20 x 16.5cm) strip in WW

▸ One 5in (13cm) square in WW –
  cut in half across the diagonal to
  make two pieces

▸ One 4in (10cm) square in WW –
  cut in half across the diagonal to
  make two pieces

▸ Six 4 x 2in (10 x 5cm) strips in WW

▸ Two 9 x 1½in (23 x 4cm) strips in Fab B

▸ One 8 x 1in (20.5 x 2.5cm) strip in Fab B

▸ One 3⅜in (8.5cm) square in Fab D

▸ One 2in (5cm) square in Fab E

▸ One 3⅜ x 2in (8.5 x 5cm) strip in Fab E

▸ Two 2in (5cm) squares in Fab F

▸ Two 3⅜ x 2in (8.5 x 5cm) strip in Fab F

1. Start by creating the V-shaped flowers: stitch the short, right-hand end of a 4 x 2in (10 x 5cm) WW strip to a 2in (5cm) Fab E square (see the left-hand unit in **Fig. A**). Next, stitch the short right-hand side of the 3⅜ x 2in (8.5 x 5cm) Fab E strip to a 4 x 2in (10 x 5cm) WW strip (see the right-hand unit in **Fig. A**). Together, these make Set 1. Repeat with the remaining 4 x 2in (10 x 5cm) WW strips, 2in (5cm) Fab F squares and 3⅜ x 2in (8.5 x 5cm) Fab F strips to make Sets 2 and 3.

2. Create the top flowerhead by stitching the diagonal edges of the 5in (13cm) WW triangles to two adjacent sides of the 3⅜in (8.5cm) Fab D square. Since both triangles are larger than the square, you'll need to match the centre of each long edge of the triangles to the centre of each square side, and the second seam should overlap and extend into the right-hand side of the first WW triangle. Rotate the unit so it's on its point and the WW triangles are at the top, then trim the ends of the WW triangles that are in line with the lower edges of the square (**Fig. B**). Do not trim across the top.

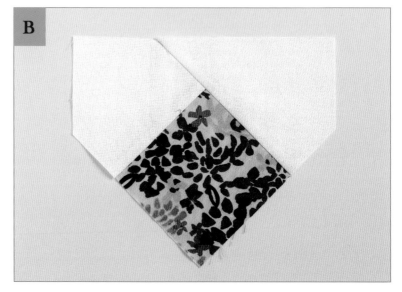

C

3. If necessary, rotate the sets made in Step 1 so they're on point. Add the left-hand side of Set 1 to the bottom-left side of the flowerhead and corner triangle, followed by the right-hand side. Add Sets 2 and 3 in the same way. Next, trim the width of the unit to 6½in (16.5cm) – to do this, place the 3¼in (8.5cm) mark on your ruler down the middle of the flower points and trim each side. Add the 4in (10cm) WW triangles to the two lower edges, then trim the whole flowerhead unit to measure 11¼in (28.5cm) tall, ensuring you have a ¼in (5mm) seam allowance below the lowest point (**Fig. C**).

4. Create the stem and leaves unit: following the technique on page 45, make up a straight stem with the 8 x 1in (20.5 x 2.5cm) Fab B strip. Prepare the leaves in the same way with the two 9 x 1½in 23 x 4cm) Fab B strips, then cut these two strips in half to make four pieces in total. To help with placement, crease the 7¾ x 6½in (20 x 16.5cm) WW background fabric in half vertically to start with. From the top, position the ends of the higher leaves 1in (2.5cm) down from each side edge and 2¾in (7cm) down from centre-top edge. The two lower leaves are positioned 1½in (4cm) below the top leaves. Trim the leaves where they meet up in the centre so they butt together then glue or baste/tack them into position before top-stitching along the longest edges. Lay the stem pieces down the centre of the background fabric, covering the raw edges of the leaves in the centre, then stitch down in the same way as the leaves (**Fig. D**).

5. Sew the stem and leaves unit to the bottom of the flowerhead unit to complete the block.

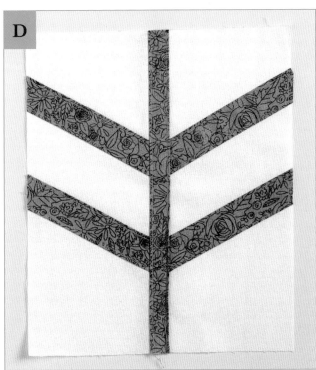

D

CENTRE PANEL 2

UNFINISHED SIZE
24½ x 8½in (62.5 x 21.5cm)

TECHNIQUE
Raw Edge Appliqué
(see page 38)

WHAT YOU NEED
▸ Fabric adhesive sheets

▸ Templates and placement diagram
(see page 176)

▸ One 18½ x 6½in (47 x 16.5cm) strip
in WW

▸ Scraps of Fab A, Fab B, Fab F and Fab G

▸ Sew-in interfacing or very thin paper,
for satin stitching

1. Following Steps 1 and 2 of the technique on page 38, prepare your appliqué shapes and fabrics as follows: 10 large petals (Fab A), four flower centres (Fab G), six small petals (Fab A), four large leaves (Fab B), six small leaves (Fab B), and four heart-shaped buds (Fab F). Note that you do not need to add a seam allowance to these shapes.

2. Referring to the placement diagram on page 176, mark the stem and appliqué positions on the 18½ x 6½in (47 x 16.5cm) WW strip. Note: the two flower designs are exactly the same; it's just each one starts from either end of the WW fabric.

3. Place pieces of interfacing or thin paper on the WS of the WW fabric, behind where the stems sit, and pin or baste/tack in place. Following the marked lines, sew satin stitch (narrow zigzag stitch) along the shorter stems first, followed by the longer stems. Gently remove the interfacing or thin paper either side of the satin stitching.

4. Referring to the photograph of the finished block, left, to help with order of placement, and following Steps 3 and 4 of the technique on page 38, fuse the appliqué leaves, flowers and hearts over the stems. Secure around the outer edges with zigzag stitch to finish.

Close-up of the Centre Panel 2 block on the finished quilt
(see opposite for instructions on making the block).

BASKET 4

UNFINISHED SIZE

12½in (32cm) square

TECHNIQUES

Single Half Square Triangle
(see page 19)

Two-in-One Half Square Triangles
(see page 19)

Raw Edge Appliqué
(see page 38)

WHAT YOU NEED

As there are several pieces in this
block, we've grouped the cutting
details into sections.

APPLIQUÉ:

▶ Fabric adhesive sheets

▶ Templates (see page 175)

▶ Scraps of Fab B

▶ Scraps of Fab D

HANDLE:

▶ One 3½ x 1½in (9 x 4cm) strip in
Fab A

▶ One 1½in (4cm) square in Fab A

▶ One 1½in (4cm) square in Fab F

BASKET:

▶ Two 1½in (4cm) squares in WW

▶ One 10½ x 2½in (27 x 6.5cm) strip in
Fab A

▶ One 10½ x 2in (27 x 5cm) strip in
Fab A

▶ One 6 x 1in (15.5 x 2.5cm) strip in
Fab A

▶ One 3 x 1in (8 x 2.5cm) strip in Fab A

▶ One 1in (2.5cm) square in Fab A

▶ One 2 x 1in (5 x 2.5cm) strip in Fab F

▶ One 1in (2.5cm) square in Fab F

▶ One 16 x 1½in (41 x 4cm) strip in
Fab G

▶ One 16 x 1½in (41 x 4cm) strip in
Fab H

LEFT BOW:

▶ One 5 x 2in (13 x 5cm) strip in WW

▶ One 3½ x 2in (9 x 5cm) strip in WW

▶ One 3 x 2½in (8 x 6.5cm) strip in WW

▶ One 2½in (6.5cm) square in WW

▶ One 2in (5cm) square in WW

▶ One 2½in (6.5cm) square in Fab F

▶ One 2in (5cm) square in Fab F

RIGHT BOW:

▶ One 5 x 2½in (13 x 6.5cm) strip in WW

▶ One 2½in (6.5cm) square in WW

▶ Two 3½ x 2in (9 x 5cm) strips in WW

▶ One 2½in (6.5cm) square in Fab F

OUTER BLOCK EDGES:

▶ One 10½ x 1½in (27 x 4cm) strip
in WW

▶ Two 12½ x 1½in (32 x 4cm) strips
in WW

A

1. Create the basket, starting with the bottom section: draw a diagonal line on the WS of two 1½in (4cm) WW squares then position them over the bottom corners of the 10½ x 2½in (27 x 6.5cm) Fab A strip, the diagonal lines running from the sides to the bottom edges. Stitch across the diagonal lines, press the seams towards the WW fabric then trim the seam allowance to ¼in (5mm) – see the bottom of **Fig. A**.

2. For the middle of the basket, we'll make a checkerboard unit. Stitch the two 16 x 1½in (41 x 4cm) Fab G and Fab H strips together lengthways, then cut into ten 1½in (4cm) wide units. Alternating the colourways, join these units together in pairs first, then stitch the pairs together – see the middle of **Fig. A**.

3. For the top of the basket, there is a 10½ x 2in (27 x5cm) Fab A strip with a narrow pieced section on top. To create this pieced section, start by making a Single Half Square Triangle unit with the 1in (2.5cm) Fab A and Fab F squares, following the technique on page 19. With the diagonal running from top left to bottom right, sandwich this unit between the 2 x 1in (5 x 2.5cm) Fab F strip on the left and the 3 x 1in (8 x 2.5cm) Fab A strip on the right, and stitch these together. Add the 6 x 1in (15.5 x 2.5cm) Fab A strip to the left of the 2 x 1in (5 x 2.5cm) Fab F strip to finish the row – see the top of **Fig. A**.

4. Join the sections in Step 1–3 to complete the basket/lower half of the block (**Fig. A**).

Continued > > >

B

5. The top half of the block is made up of three units, so let's start with the left bow on the left-hand side of the handle. Following the technique on page 19, make two Single Half Square Triangles – one with 2½in (6.5cm) WW and Fab F squares, and one with the 2in (5cm) WW and Fab F squares. With the diagonal running from top left to bottom right, stitch the larger Half Square Triangle to the right-hand side of the 3 x 2½in (8 x 6.5cm) WW strip. With the diagonal running from top right to bottom left, stitch the small Half Square Triangle to the right-hand side of the 3½ x 2in (9 x 5cm) WW strip. Join these two units together, with the large Half Square Triangle unit on top. Add the 5 x 2in (13 x 5cm) WW strip to the top of the joined units to finish the left bow unit (see the left-hand side of **Fig. B**).

6. For the right bow, on the right-hand side of the handle unit, begin by making two Half Square Triangles with the 2½in (6.5cm) WW and Fab F squares, following the Two-in-One Half Square Triangles technique on page 19. Trim all units to 1½in (4cm) square if necessary. With the diagonal running from top left to bottom right, stitch one Half Square Triangle to the left-hand side of the 3½ x 2in (9 x 5cm) WW strip. Repeat with the second Half Square Triangle, this time with the diagonal running in the opposite direction. Stitch these pieces together, with the second unit on top, then add the 5 x 2½in (13 x 6.5cm) strip to the top of the unit to complete the right bow (see the right-hand side of **Fig. B**).

7. To make the handle, first stitch one short end of the 3½ x 1½in (9 x 4cm) Fab A strip to the top of the 1½in (4cm) Fab F square. Sew the 1½in (4cm) Fab A square to the bottom of the 1½in (4cm) Fab F square (see the middle of **Fig. B**).

8. Join the three units made in Steps 5–7, with the handle in the middle, to complete the handle/top half of the block (**Fig. B**).

9. Stitch together the two halves made in the previous steps. Add the 10½ x 1½in (27 x 4cm) WW strip to the top, then sew the two 12½ x 1½in (32 x 4cm) strips to either side.

10. Referring to the photograph of the finished block on page 140 for placement, and following the technique on page 38, prepare and fuse the appliqué bird (Fab B) and heart (Fab D) shapes either side of the bows. Stitch around these shapes with your chosen stitch (we used zigzag stitch) to complete the block.

CURVED PIECING 2

UNFINISHED SIZE

12½in (32cm) square

TECHNIQUES

Curved Piecing
(see page 36)

WHAT YOU NEED

▶ Templates (see page 171)

▶ Template A (quarter circle) – cut two in each of all eight fabrics

▶ Template B ('frame') – cut twelve in WW and one each in Fab A, C, D and E

I. Referring to the technique on page 36, start by creating the following units:

▶ Two in Fab A (template 1) and WW (template 2)
▶ One in Fab B (template 1) and WW (template 2)
▶ One in Fab B (template 1) and Fab E (template 2)
▶ Two in Fab C (template 1) and WW (template 2)
▶ Two in Fab D (template 1) and WW (template 2)
▶ Two in Fab E (template 1) and WW (template 2)
▶ One in Fab F (template 1) and WW (template 2)
▶ One in Fab F (template 1) and Fab D (template 2)
▶ One in Fab G (template 1) and WW (template 2)
▶ One in Fab G (template 1) and Fab C (template 2)
▶ One in Fab H (template 1) and WW (template 2)
▶ One in Fab H (template 1) and Fab A (template 2).

2. Arrange the units in the layout seen in the photograph of the finished block above. Pay attention to the order of the units and their rotation – it's easy to make a mistake here! Stitch the units together in rows of four, then stitch the rows in pairs before stitching all of them together to complete the block. Press the seams of the rows open, to avoid bulk.

TALL BIRD 2

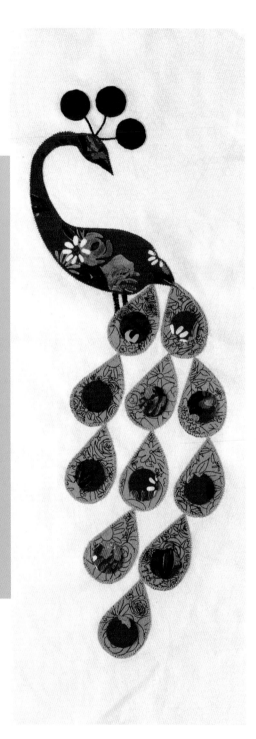

UNFINISHED SIZE

18½ x 6½in (47 x 16.5cm)

TECHNIQUE

Raw Edge Appliqué
(see page 38)

Appliqué with Freezer Paper
(see page 41)

WHAT YOU NEED

▸ Templates (see page 176)

▸ Fabric adhesive sheets

▸ Freezer paper

▸ Thin card

▸ One 18½ x 6½in (47 x 16.5cm) strip
  in WW

▸ One 7 x 5in (18 x 13cm) strip in Fab A

▸ One 5 x 4¼in (13 x 11.5cm) strip in Fab A

▸ One 5 x 9in (13 x 22cm) strip in Fab B

▸ Scraps in Fab G

I. Following Steps 1 and 2 on page 38, prepare the following appliqué shapes and fabrics: peacock body (Fab A), 11 tail feathers (Fab B). Prepare the tail feather circles (Fab A) and head plume (Fab G) following the technique on page 41.

2. Position the peacock body over the 18½ x 6½in (47 x 16.5cm) WW strip, its head 3in (8cm) down from the top and the neck ¾in (2cm) in from the left-hand edge, as shown in the photograph of the finished block opposite. Fuse then appliqué in place (we used zigzag stitch). Sew three satin stitch (narrow zigzag stitch) lines that radiate from the head, each approx. ¾in (2cm) tall, then appliqué a plume circle over the end of each line with your chosen stitch (we used slip stitch), covering them slightly (**Fig. A**).

3. Sew two black satin stitch legs below the bird body. Referring to the photograph of the finished block opposite, arrange the rows of tail feathers below the body, positioning them at slightly jaunty angles to suggest movement (**Fig. B**). The lowest feather is approx. 2in (5cm) up from the bottom of the WW background. When you're happy, fuse then appliqué the feathers in place with your chosen stitch (we used zigzag stitch). To finish, appliqué the tail circles over the centres of the tail feathers with your chosen stitch (we used slip stitch).

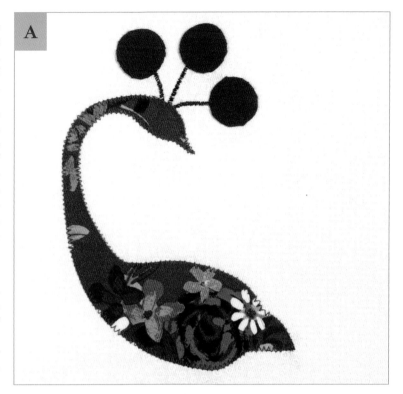

ASSEMBLY, QUILTING & FINISHING

Once you've made all your blocks, you're ready to stitch them together and begin making up the final quilt. Ensure all your blocks have been well pressed with no twisted seam allowances.

On the following pages, you'll see how to assemble and stitch the blocks together, make your quilt sandwich, quilt the final design and then bind the edges for a neat finish.

If you're a beginner, we would encourage you to make up your quilt in the same way we have; however, once you have the core techniques established – or if you're a more confident quilter – there's no reason why you can't adjust the quilt layout, add a border or use a different binding method!

QUILT LAYOUT

	WEEK 12: Heart 4	WEEK 2: Heart 1	WEEK 10: Heart 3	WEEK 28: Heart 6	WEEK 34: Heart 7	WEEK 5: Heart 2	WEEK 38: Heart 8	WEEK 18: Heart 5	
WEEK 46: Flying Geese 4	**WEEK 40:** Basket 2		**WEEK 8:** Log Cabin 1		**WEEK 35:** Large Pieced Block 2		**WEEK 29:** Basket 1		**WEEK 30:** Flying Geese 2

| | | | | WEEK 14: Bird 2 | WEEK 37: Bird 4 | WEEK 25: Bird 3 | | | |

WEEK 48: Tall Flower 4

WEEK 15: Dresden 1

WEEK 52: Tall Bird 2

WEEK 51: Curving Piecing 2

WEEK 24: Tall Flower 2

WEEK 44: Bird 5

WEEK 47: English Paper Piecing 2

WEEK 9: Centre Panel 1

WEEK 49: Centre Panel 2

WEEK 6: Bird 1

WEEK 19: English Paper Piecing 1

WEEK 43: Small Flower 5

WEEK 39: Tall Flower 3

WEEK 26: Small Flower 4

WEEK 22: Tall Bird 1

WEEK 17: Tall Flower 1

WEEK 27: Curved Piecing 1

WEEK 41: Dresden 2

| WEEK 4: Small Flower 1 | WEEK 20: Small Flower 2 | WEEK 21: Small Flower 3 |

| **WEEK 1:** Flying Geese 1 | **WEEK 45:** Basket 3 | | **WEEK 11:** Large Pieced Block 1 | | **WEEK 33:** Log Cabin 2 | | **WEEK 50:** Basket 4 | | **WEEK 36:** Flying Geese 3 |

| WEEK 3: Star 1 | WEEK 42: Star 8 | WEEK 16: Star 4 | WEEK 31: Star 6 | WEEK 7: Star 2 | WEEK 13: Star 3 | WEEK 32: Star 7 | WEEK 23: Star 5 |

QUILT ASSEMBLY

Creating the sections

TOP PANEL (RED) – 14 BLOCKS

1. Stitch the eight 6½in (16.5cm) square blocks together in the order shown in the diagram opposite.

2. Stitch the four 12½in (32cm) square blocks together in the order shown in the diagram opposite.

3. Stitch these two strips of blocks together, with the strip of smaller blocks along the top.

4. Add the two Flying Geese blocks to either side, as shown in the diagram opposite.

BOTTOM PANEL (PURPLE) – 14 BLOCKS

Repeat the process detailed for the top (red) panel, except in Step 3 stitch the strip of small blocks along the bottom.

LEFT PANEL (YELLOW) – 5 BLOCKS

1. Stitch the three 12½in (32cm) blocks together in the order shown in the diagram opposite.

2. Stitch the two Tall Flower blocks together in the order shown in the diagram opposite.

3. Stitch these two strips of blocks together with the Tall Flower blocks on the left-hand side.

RIGHT PANEL (BLUE) – 5 BLOCKS

Repeat the process detailed for the left (yellow) panel, except in Step 3 stitch the Tall Flower blocks on the right-hand side.

CENTRE PANEL (GREEN) – 14 BLOCKS

1. Stitch together the Tall Bird 2 block and the three 6½in (16.5cm) Small Flower blocks below it (Small Flower 5, 4 and 1) in the order shown in the diagram opposite.

2. Stitch together the Tall Bird 1 block and the three 6½in (16.5cm) Bird blocks above it (Bird 1, 5 and 3) in the order shown in the diagram opposite.

3. Stitch the two centre panels together. Sew the Bird 2 and Bird 4 blocks together, then sew the Small Flower 2 and Small Flower 3 blocks together. Stitch these pairs to the top and bottom of the joined centre panels – the joined Bird blocks along the top and the joined Small Flower blocks along the bottom.

4. Stitch the two units made in Steps 1 and 2 to either side of the centre panel.

Joining the sections

Lay out your five panels in the arrangement shown in the diagram opposite. Stitch the left and right panels to either side of the centre panel before adding the top and bottom panels to complete the construction.

QUILT SANDWICH

This is a term you'll hear a lot in the world of quilting. A quilt sandwich is simply made up of a quilt backing, your newly stitched quilt top and a layer of batting/wadding in between the two. This sandwich is what gives padding, depth and warmth to your quilt.

The batting/wadding and backing should be 3–4in (8–10cm) larger than your quilt top; for this book's quilt, this means your backing and batting/wadding pieces will need to be 76 x 64in (193 x 162cm). This extra fabric allows for any 'shrinkage' or fabric shift when quilting.

Assembling the sandwich

1. Press the backing fabric then place it right side (RS) facing down. The reason you press the backing fabric is to make sure it is flat and smooth – it may help to tape the fabric to a flat surface with masking tape to keep it crease-free when you add the other layers.

2. Your batting/wadding should be around the same size as the backing fabric. Place this on top, patting out any wrinkles.

3. Your quilt top then goes centrally on top of the batting/wadding, RS facing up. At this point, it is worth checking that there are no thread tails on the back of your quilt top – these may show through or create little lumps on the RS of the fabric.

From left to right:
quilt top, batting/wadding,
backing fabric.

Curved safety pins used for basting/tacking, spaced 3–4in (8–10cm) apart.

Basting/tacking the sandwich

Basting/tacking your quilt will stop the layers shifting as you sew, so it's worth taking the time to make sure they are secure, flat and wrinkle free. There are several ways to hold your quilt sandwich together before quilting, so choose whichever works best for you.

◊ **Pins:** Curved safety pins are ideal for basting/tacking your quilt sandwich, as their shape allows you to scoop up the three layers in one fell swoop.

To use them, your quilt sandwich should ideally be on a flat surface. Start either on one side or in the centre, and pin every 3–4in (8–10cm) or a hand-width apart. It's a good idea to avoid pinning over the lines you'll be sewing if possible, so that the pins can remain in place while quilting. Try to pin in a grid so the pins can be easily spotted for removal after quilting!

You can also buy a special tool which will help you to close the quilter's safety pins, which avoids bunching up the quilt sandwich and prevents sore fingers!

◊ **Spray basting/tacking:** Using a basting/tacking spray is a quick method as there are no pins or stitches to remove after quilting. Make sure your spray has been specifically designed to be used with fabric, as this won't damage your sewing machine and can be washed out after the quilt is finished.

Choose a space that is well ventilated. Spray your batting/wadding lightly on one side then lay your backing fabric on top, RS up, smoothing out any wrinkles as you go. Spray the wrong side (WS) of your quilt top and lay it centrally over the batting/wadding again, RS up and smoothing out any wrinkles or puckers. With larger quilts it may be easier to spray half or a quarter of the fabric at a time.

Try to avoid spraying the surrounding area. If you are concerned, lay down a few paper sheets around your quilt.

◊ **Thread basting/tacking:** Many quilters prefer this method as you're automatically smoothing the fabrics as you sew. Cotton thread is most commonly used, although polyester thread is easy to pull through when removing the stitches. If you will wash your quilt after its finished, you could use water-soluble thread for basting/tacking: this will dissolve in water, and mean you don't need to unpick your stitches after quilting.

Use a long needle and a long piece of thread – that way, there is no need to knot. Start in the centre of your quilt and make large stitches to the outer edge of the quilt. Go back to the centre and sew to the opposite edge, then at 90 degrees. Continue across the quilt in this way to form a grid.

Some sewing machines have an extra long basting/tacking stitch, which you may find useful.

A lot of quilters use a combination of spraying first then basting/tacking to ensure the quilt sandwich is firmly held together while it's being quilted.

◊ Also available are **quilter's basting guns:** These shoot a plastic tack through the layers of your sandwich which you snip away with small scissors after quilting. Be careful not to sew through the tacks as these will damage your needle. It's worth noting the gun's nose may leave holes in finer fabrics.

◊ **Fusible webbing or adhesive sheets** are a quick alternative if you have used a sew-in batting/wadding. Lay a piece of webbing or an adhesive sheet either side of the batting/wadding before pressing all three layers of your quilt sandwich together.

QUILTING

Once your quilted layers are basted/tacked in place, you're ready to start quilting!

There are many ways to quilt. You can do it by hand, either with hand stitches or tying; this can be quite time-consuming, especially if you're working on a larger quilt, but can be relaxing, methodical and, of course, a quiet practice as you don't need a machine. If you choose to machine quilt there are so many styles: free-motion embroidery, stitch-in-the-ditch, echo and machine stitching with stencils. We'll look at these on the following pages.

Your quilting design can be anything you like – circles, swirls, geometric patterns or loose straight lines, there are no rules! But remember the point of quilting is primarily to hold the quilt sandwich together, so an even pattern with no large, unsewn areas works best. If you are a beginner quilter, you're probably not going to exhibit your work or put it into competitions, so please don't worry about perfection. You're meant to enjoy the sewing process, and nobody is going to notice the odd uneven or wobbly stitch! If it's all a little daunting, there's always the professional long arm quilter who will quilt your quilt for you.

Thread-wise, for machine quilting we like to use a 50–60wt cotton thread; use a finer thread if you want the stitches to sink more into the work, or heavier weight thread to make the stitches bolder. We use the same weight of thread in the top and bottom of the sewing machine. If you would

like to quilt by hand, for delicate stitching you can use a fine 28wt hand-quilting thread; for a bolder look, we recommend 12wt cotton thread or 8–12wt cotton perle thread. However, if you're worried about your stitches showing on plain backing fabric, you could use bobbin fill thread as an alternative: this is a lightweight thread that sinks into your fabric, and a little goes a long way.

Quilting needles have a slim point and a strong shaft to cope with multiple layers of fabric. Generally we use a 90/14 needle in the sewing machine. If you're quilting by hand, you will need special quilting needles, called 'Betweens'. For fine quilting, use either a size 10 or 12 Betweens; for bolder quilting, use a size 6 Betweens or a size 22 Chenille needle.

After you have finished quilting, you can trim the backing fabric and batting/wadding back to the size of the quilt top, ready for binding. When you trim your quilt, make sure the corners have 90 degree angles exactly; this ensures neat, bound corners later.

Marking guidelines

MARKING TOOLS

Whether you're free-hand drawing or using templates and rulers, there are lots of marking products to choose from! Below are the ones we use most often.

◊ **Air-erasable pens (Fig. A)** use ink that disappears after around 24 hours. Don't use these on a project that takes a few days to complete! Be careful not to iron over your markings, as the ink becomes permanent.

◊ **Water-erasable pens (Fig. A)** use ink that is removed with a damp cloth or washing. Like the air-erasable pens, make sure you don't iron over the ink to avoid setting it permanently.

◊ **Chalk (Fig. B)** is available in block or pen form and comes in many colours. Its benefit is that it brushes away easily, but this is not ideal for hand sewing – as the fabric passes through your hands, the chalk lines can disappear.

◊ **Heat-erasable pens (Fig. C)** use an ink that disappears when ironed or rubbed. Always test these pens on a spare piece of the fabric you're using, as sometimes they can bleach the fabric. This is not a problem if you're marking within the seam allowance, but you need to be careful with these if you're marking quilting lines on your fabric. Avoid using heat-erasable pens when hand quilting; the heat from your hands can make the lines disappear as you sew – we learnt this from experience!

◊ **Quilt pounces (Fig. D)** are chalk-filled pads that are used with stencils. Different colours of chalk are available to help your design stand out no matter what colour fabric you're using.

Air-erasable pen (left) and water-erasable pen (right).

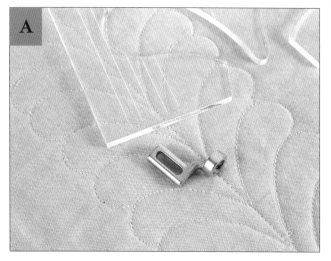

USING STENCILS

Marking your quilting design with templates is an easy and effective way of achieving perfectly quilted patterns. There are hundreds to choose from!

◊ **Acrylic templates (Fig. A)** that work with specially designed presser feet are available, and they allow you to sew your pattern around the templates without the need for marking. The presser feet look like a free-motion/darning foot but without the spring, so they don't 'hop' as a free-motion feet would. Follow the manufacturer's instructions; many have video tutorials which will help you to get the most out of the templates.

◊ With **plastic templates (Fig. B)** you'll need to mark your fabric. On smaller pieces you can use air- or water-erasable ink pens, chalk pens or fabric pencils. Use your free-motion/darning foot on your sewing machine, and simply sew over the lines!

On larger projects you'll find it quicker to use a quilt pounce (**Fig. C**). Place the template over the fabric and sweep the pad across the top. Move the template to the next position, matching the pattern, and repeat.

◊ **Paper patterns** will need to be traced either directly onto your fabric, or onto quilters' paper, which can then be torn away after sewing.

If you have a large project or intend to use these patterns frequently, it may be worth investing in a light box. Simply place the pattern on the box, your fabric right side up on top, and use any of your marking tools to trace the design.

If a light box isn't an option, tape the pattern to a window on a sunny day; alternatively, a glass-topped table with a lamp underneath works a treat!

Machine quilting

This is the quickest way to quilt, and typically will leave you with very neat, accurate results.

At the end of the quilting, or if you need to change thread, take a needle and pull the bottom thread to the top. Loop the top and bottom threads together in a loose knot, place the needle through the loop and push the knot until it sits on the top of the fabric. Thread the ends through the needle, take the needle into the fabric just under the knot, and feed it in between the layers by about an inch (2.5cm), then bring it back to the top. Gently pull the thread until the knot pops inside the quilt and is hidden from view. Trim the thread.

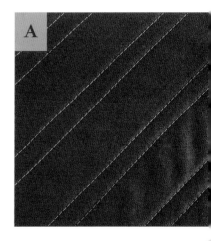

STRAIGHT-LINE QUILTING

Just as the name suggests, straight line quilting is sewing straight lines across your quilt. We recommend creating guidelines to follow. For straight lines, you can use either a ruler and fabric marker pen or chalk; a seam guide on your machine (this slots into the back of your walking foot); or lay strips of masking tape across your quilt top and sew alongside them. (This is a quick way to quilt lines, but try not to catch the tape with your stitches – it can be difficult to remove from under the stitch! Guess how we found out...)

Some straight-line quilting designs include parallel straight lines (**Fig. A**), which look particularly impressive when stitched diagonally across the whole quilt; cross-hatching (**Fig. B**), which involves sewing a second set of straight lines that run at either 90- or 60-degree angles to your initial set of straight lines; and abstract lines (**Fig. C**), which are perfect if you're not confident with sewing parallel straight lines.

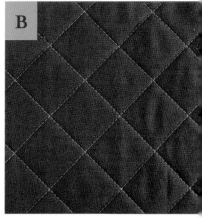

ECHO QUILTING

This is a simple technique of outlining or sewing inside blocks or appliqué shapes either by hand or machine. It gives a very modern look to your work and is a great way of filling empty spaces.

The outlines don't necessarily need to be marked out, making this a quick method of adding texture and interest to your quilt. If you're machine sewing this can be done using either your quarter-inch foot or the edge of your standard or walking foot. When pivoting around corners and curves, leave the needle in the 'down' position so that your stitch line is fluid. Many machines have a 'needle up/down' function, which is invaluable in this case. However, if you are sewing lots of curves and angles on your sewing machine, try free-motion embroidery with a free-motion foot.

Sew as many echoing lines as you like – you can fill in the whole space or simply create a couple of outlines (**Fig. D**).

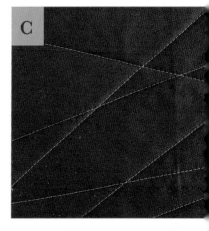

FREE-MOTION QUILTING

This is a particularly favourite method of Debbie's, and is an excellent way of adding texture and interesting shapes to your quilt top.

◊ Think of your needle and thread as a pen and ink, but instead of moving the pen over the paper, you move the fabric under the needle to create your own unique designs.

◊ You will need a drop feed dog facility for your sewing machine (the feed dogs are the teeth that carry the fabric through the machine; by dropping these out of the way, you have control over moving the fabric in any direction you like) or a darning plate to cover the feed dogs, making them inactive. You'll also need a free-motion/darning foot. This foot 'hops' across the fabric, and allows you to see where you're stitching.

◊ Have your machine set on a straight stitch with your needle in the centre position. The length of the stitch depends on how quickly you move your fabric – the quicker you move it, the longer the stitch you will sew. Hold the fabric either side of the needle, foot on the pedal and then off you go!

◊ Try to keep the stitches as even as you can across the fabric. It's always helpful to practise first on scrap fabric.

◊ Try to start sewing at the edge of your quilt to keep the ends of the thread out of the way.

◊ Posture is important, particularly when you're sewing for a while. Sit with your shoulders back and your elbows ideally at the same level as your machine. It's tempting to hunch your shoulders over your work, but you could suffer later. So, relax and enjoy the free-motion experience!

◊ Free-motion designs include stippling, also known as Vermicelli stitching (seen in the example, right), which is simply stitching meandering lines across your quilt; another idea is to stitch around motifs within your quilt (which is similar to echo quilting on the previous page but is more free-hand).

STITCH-IN-THE-DITCH QUILTING

This method entails sewing over an existing seam (the 'ditch') in your quilt top to create a barely visible stitch line, allowing the fabric and piecing of your project to be the main focus of the quilt. As the stitches are not meant to be seen, many quilters choose an invisible, monofilament thread to thread through their machine, or a colour thread that matches the fabric.

You can use a regular sewing machine foot or walking (dual-/even-feed) foot to stitch in the ditch, or you could invest in a stitch-in-the-ditch foot, which has a blade-like guide along the centre.

Use your fingers to feel which way the seams have been pressed – one side of the fabric will be slightly raised, which creates the 'ditch' for you to sew along. When sewing, place your hands either side of the seam and gently pull them apart to open out the seam to give you a better guide line. As the stitches aren't creating a seam, it may be preferable to increase your stitch length to 3.

Do check the manufacturer's instructions on the batting/ wadding packaging for a guide on how far apart to sew your seams, to make sure your quilt sandwich will hold together. The quilting distance can vary from 3in (8cm) to 10in (25.5cm), depending on the fibre content and how you're going to use your quilt. For a large quilt like ours, you may need to add a few extra rows of stitches over your work to keep the quilt layers together.

Hand quilting

Straight line, cross-hatch, echo quilting – all of these quilting techniques can be hand-sewn. It takes longer than machine sewing, but it's a perfect way to relax without the noise of a sewing machine and the results are worth the time taken.

◊ Ideally your stitches should be uniform, measuring ¼in (5mm) in length or smaller. If your work is being judged in a quilt show it's expected that your stitches are small and even on both sides of your work. However, for your own quilt, size and uniformity of the stitches is entirely up to you. Personally, we like to see a few uneven stitches as we believe they add to a quilt's personality, and shows that it really has been hand-quilted! If it's important for you to achieve perfection then take your time and practise. If not, then just enjoy the process and be proud of your work, no matter how uneven your stitches are!

◊ A few things you'll need for the best results are hand-quilting thread, Betweens, a quilting hoop or frame and a thimble. Hand-quilting thread is quite heavy and is coated to enable the thread to travel through your quilt sandwich easily. Alternatively, try waxing your thread using a beeswax block.

◊ Quilting hoops are deeper than embroidery hoops, making them stronger and able to take the weight of fabric. Also available are lap and floor frames. Like the hoops, a lap frame is ideal for smaller, on-the-go designs; floor frames are perfect for larger quilts.

◊ We like to use a leather thimble for hand quilting, but you may find a metal or rubber one easier to use. It's your choice!

TYING A QUILTER'S KNOT

This is the easiest and quickest knot you'll ever tie! It makes a neat knot at the end of your thread and, depending on the number of wraps you make, you can create any size knot with ease.

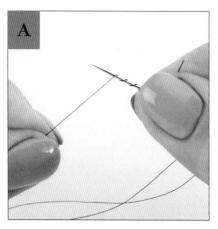
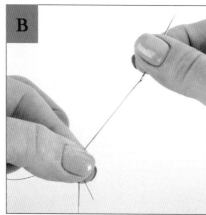
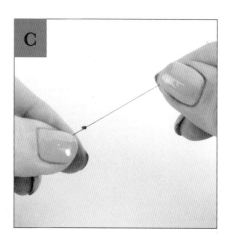

I. Thread your needle then bend the shorter end of the thread so it points towards the eye of the needle. Wrap the longer end of the thread around the needle three or four times (**Fig. A**) – the more wraps, the larger the knot will be.

2. Hold on to the wrapped threads and pull the needle through (**Fig. B**).

3. Take the wrapped threads to the end of the thread. You'll have a neat little knot (**Fig. C**)!

BASIC HAND-QUILTING TECHNIQUE

1. After constructing your quilt sandwich, mark out your pattern. This could be using a stencil or a free-hand design. Place your fabric into a frame or hoop but, unlike embroidery, don't have the fabric taut.

2. Tie a small quilter's knot at the end of the thread (see opposite). Insert your needle into your work from the top, around ½in (1.25cm) from where you want to start quilting. Bring the needle up again at the point where you'll begin (**Fig. A**).

3. Tug the thread sharply to pull the knot inside the batting/ wadding to hide it (see **Fig. B**).

4. You can start by just sewing individual stitches. Pop on your thimble and take the needle through from the front to the back of the quilt sandwich to start making a running stitch. When you gain a bit more confidence, you can take several stitches onto the needle by inserting the end into your work with one hand and feeling where the needle comes through under the work with the other hand. Rock the needle backwards and bring through to the top, then repeat until you have three or four stitches on your needle that are ¼in (5mm) long (**Fig. C**). At this point you can undo them if they don't look even enough. Pull the needle through and repeat!

5. When you come to your final stitch, with the needle and thread on top of your work, tie a small knot ½in (1.25cm) from the point where the thread comes through the fabric.

6. Take the needle through to the wrong side (WS) of the quilt to create the last stitch, and gently tug the knot into the batting/wadding to hide it, just as you did at the start. You're finished (**Fig. D**)!

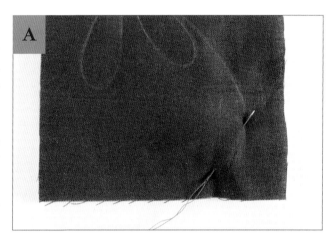

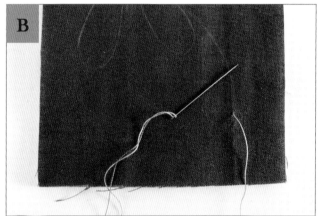

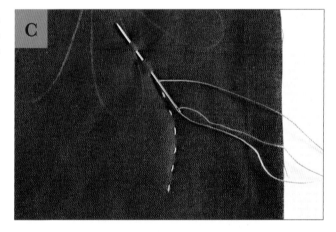

Tie quilting

If you're a beginner quilter or just want to try something different, and the thought of hand or machine quilting a large quilt is a bit daunting, you'll find this tying method quicker and easier (although it can be hard on the fingers).

Tie quilting is another method of hand finishing your quilt. With a strong thread, yarn, embroidery floss or other thread of your choice, knots are created on the top side across the quilt at regular intervals, usually 4–6in (10–15.5cm) apart, depending on your batting/wadding. Leaving short thread tails (approx. ½in or 1.5cm) on the top side of the quilt gives texture and a rustic look to your work; buttons or other embellishments can also be added to the knot to create more decoration.

I. With the top/right side of your quilt facing, insert your threaded needle through the quilt sandwich, leaving a tail of approximately 1½in (4cm). Holding onto the tail, bring the needle back up through the quilt close to your original insertion point. Repeat this one more time, ensuring the two stitches on the back are on top of each other.

2. Cut the thread, leaving a second tail of 1½in (4cm). Make a double knot, then cut the tails to approximately ½in (1.5cm) long. Repeat at intervals across the whole quilt top. You'll not only achieve a textured knot on the top of the quilt, but also a small, neat double stitch at intervals on the reverse.

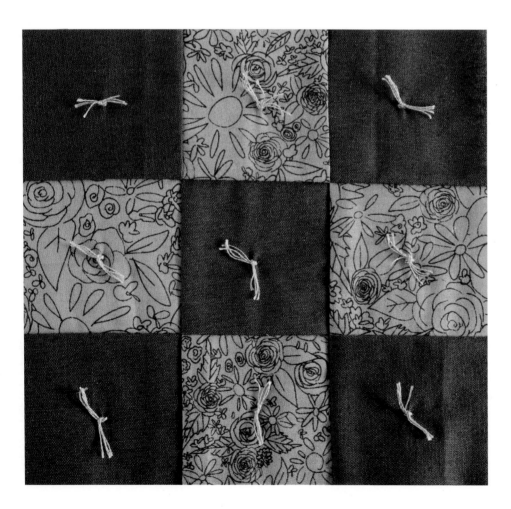

BINDING

Binding doesn't just finish the raw edge of your quilt; it creates a neat frame to your work and adds another element of design.

For a quilt, binding is often the final stage, after the sandwich has been quilted and trimmed. There are many ways of binding a quilt to give a professional finish; the method we used creates neat, mitred corners.

If you decide not to make your own (which we've covered overleaf), straight binding is available to buy in many colours, widths and prints. Single-fold straight binding will have the long edges pressed to the centre; quilt binding is folded and pressed in half wrong sides (WS) facing and with the raw edges together. For our quilt, we've made our own quilt binding.

If you wish to make your own binding, you'll need ¾yd (0.75m) length of 44in (112cm) wide fabric. You'll then cut seven 2½in (6.5cm) strips across the width of the fabric.

Note: To calculate the length of binding you need, add approximately 15in (40cm) to the total length of all four outside edges.

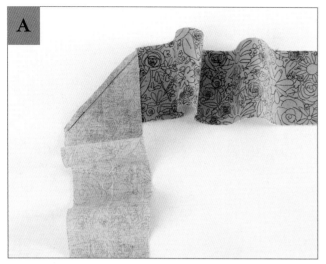

A

B

C

D

1. Place the ends of two binding strips right sides (RS) together at a 45-degree angle. Draw a diagonal line from top left to bottom right then stitch along the line. Cut off excess seam allowance (**Fig. A**) and press the seam open. Repeat to join the remaining strips in the same way. Press the binding along its entire length, wrong sides (WS) together, matching raw edges.

2. On the top of the quilt, decide where you want the final join to sit – this is usually along one side edge. Pin or mark accordingly (see the bright yellow lozenge opposite, in **Fig. E**). Leaving a long tail of binding beyond the mark (roughly 6in/16.5cm or so), line up the binding along the quilt edge, raw edges together. Clip or pin in place. Using a walking (even-/dual-feed) foot if you have one, start sewing at a point a fair distance away from the mark towards the first corner (see the dashed white line in **Fig. B**)- you need to leave a long gap between the start and finish of the binding stitching to make it easier to sew a neat join at the final stage of applying your binding.

3. To create a neat, mitred corner, sew to within ¼in (5mm) of the end, stop, back-tack/reverse stitch and remove the quilt from the machine. Fold the binding up and away from the quilt, ensuring the binding raw edges run in line with the next edge you're about to sew (**Fig. C**).

4. Fold the binding back on itself and align the fold with the raw edge you've just sewn. (**TIP:** If you make the fold ⅛in (3mm) above the raw edge, this helps to create a really flat, 45-degree mitre on the front of the quilt.) Pin or clip in place and continue to stitch from the fold (**Fig. D**).

5. Repeat the process for every corner. At the last corner, and along the final side (the first side you started stitching from), sew towards the joining mark but leave a long gap unsewn (**Fig. E**). Line up the raw edges of the binding along the edge of the quilt. On each strip, mark a point that is half the strip's width – in our case, 1¼in (3.25cm) – either side of joining mark (the yellow lozenge). Cut off the excess binding.

6. Open out the binding. With RS together, join the two strips at a 45-degree angle in the same way you joined the binding strips at the start (**Fig. F**). This is slightly tricky but manoeuvre the quilt and you'll be able to do it; the longer the unsewn gap, the easier this will be. We would suggest pinning the 45-degree angle first, to check the binding has not twisted, before you stitch. Cut off the excess seam allowance to ¼in (5mm) and press the seam open.

7. Re-fold and press the binding flat (**Fig. G**) before stitching in place to complete.

8. Press the binding away from the quilt then fold it to the reverse side. Pin or clip the binding in place, making sure it covers the line of machine stitching. The corners will naturally form a mitre. Hand-sew the binding down with slip stitch. **Fig. H** shows one mitred corner from the back; **Fig. I** shows one mitred corner from the front.

INSPIRATIONAL BLOCKS

The blocks in this quilt can be used individually to create smaller
projects such as bags and pillow covers, and can take on an
entirely different look depending on the fabrics
you choose. Here are a few ideas.

Pillow Cover (Week 4: Small Flower 1)

The cover is a repeated
design, with the four units
facing in different directions.
After making the individual
units, we added 2in (5cm)
wide border strips around
each one as the joined units
alone would have made
quite a small cover. The back
of the cover closes with a zip.

Pillow Cover (Week 35: Large Pieced Block 2)
Using just two neutral-coloured fabrics with a white fabric for this block really makes this design stand out, and creates a stunning effect. A 2½in (6.5cm) wide border was added around the edge of the block to complete the pillow front; we then made the pillow back with an envelope closure to finish it off.

Tote Bag (Week 40: Basket 2)

The size of the block dictated the size of this bag, so the block was made up first, then a border added before cutting the back and lining pieces. The corners are boxed and a foam stabilizer was used to give the bag a little rigidity.

Zipped Pouch
(Week 43: Small Flower 5)
This flower block is the perfect size to embellish a zipped cosmetic pouch! The off-set design gives the pouch a quirky look, and is balanced with a wrist handle on the opposite side. A matching ribbon threaded through the zip pull adds the finishing touch.

Place Mat
(Week 8: Log Cabin 1)
A single block in batik fabrics with a white-on-white background, this could be a single mat to pop under a plant pot or vase, or part of a matching set to dress the table. A thermal batting/ wadding would work well, backed with plain fabric, quilted then bound.

TEMPLATES

All templates provided are at 100% scale, with no need to resize. Foundation Paper Piecing templates are mirrored already, so you simply need to trace these off as is.

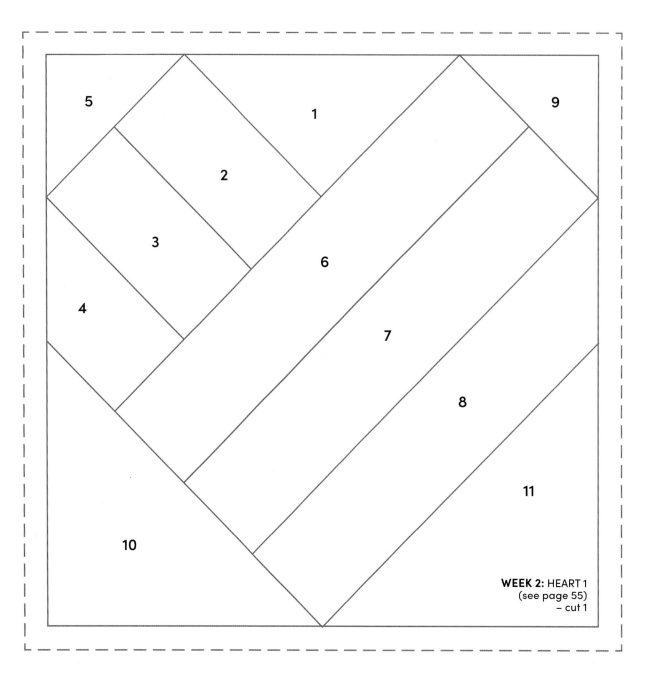

WEEK 2: HEART 1
(see page 55)
– cut 1

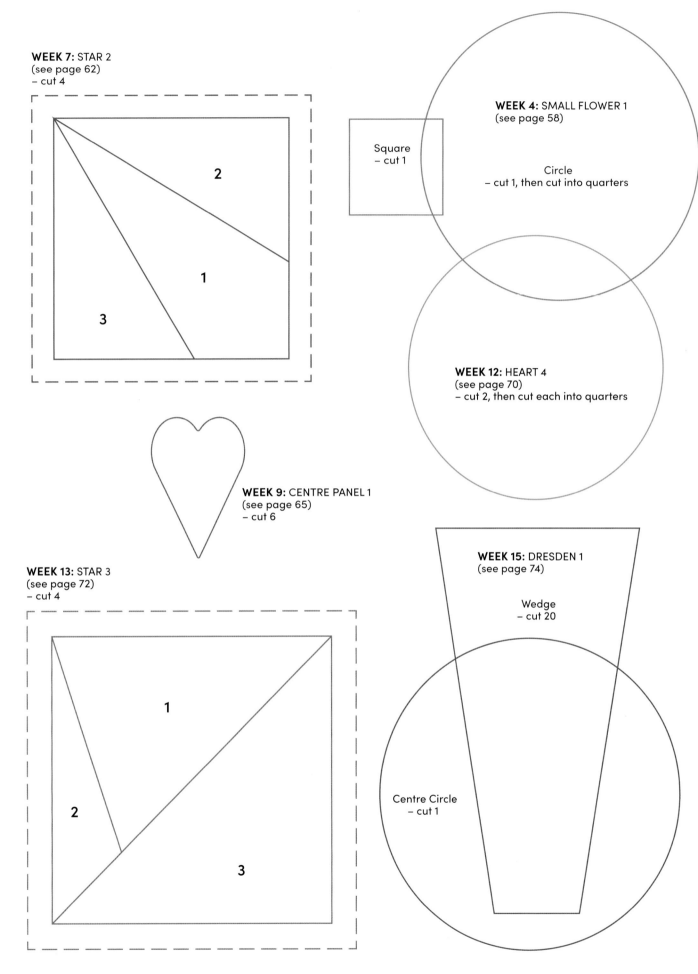

WEEK 7: STAR 2
(see page 62)
– cut 4

2

1

3

WEEK 4: SMALL FLOWER 1
(see page 58)

Square
– cut 1

Circle
– cut 1, then cut into quarters

WEEK 12: HEART 4
(see page 70)
– cut 2, then cut each into quarters

WEEK 9: CENTRE PANEL 1
(see page 65)
– cut 6

WEEK 13: STAR 3
(see page 72)
– cut 4

1

2

3

WEEK 15: DRESDEN 1
(see page 74)

Wedge
– cut 20

Centre Circle
– cut 1

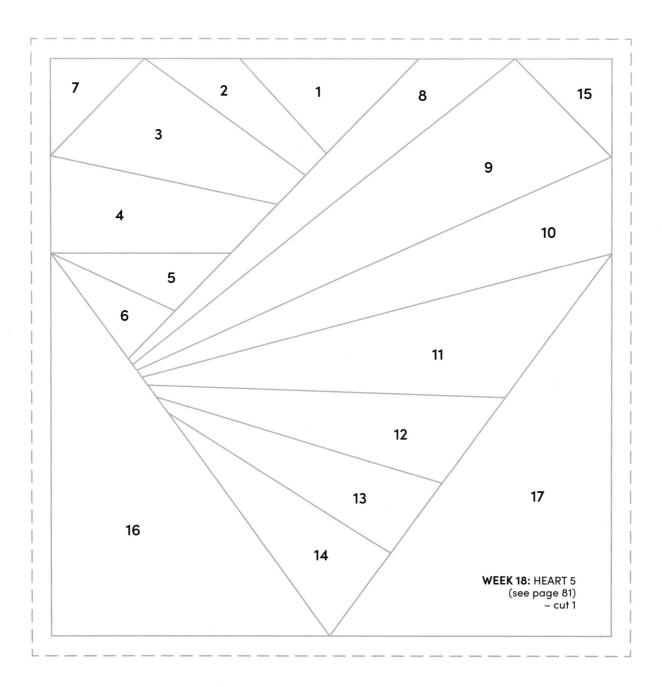

7

2

1

8

15

3

9

4

10

5

6

11

12

17

13

16

14

WEEK 18: HEART 5
(see page 81)
– cut 1

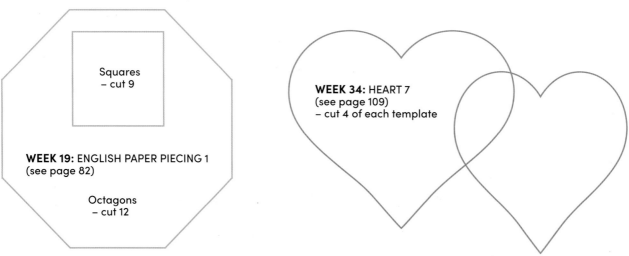

Squares
– cut 9

WEEK 19: ENGLISH PAPER PIECING 1
(see page 82)

Octagons
– cut 12

WEEK 34: HEART 7
(see page 109)
– cut 4 of each template

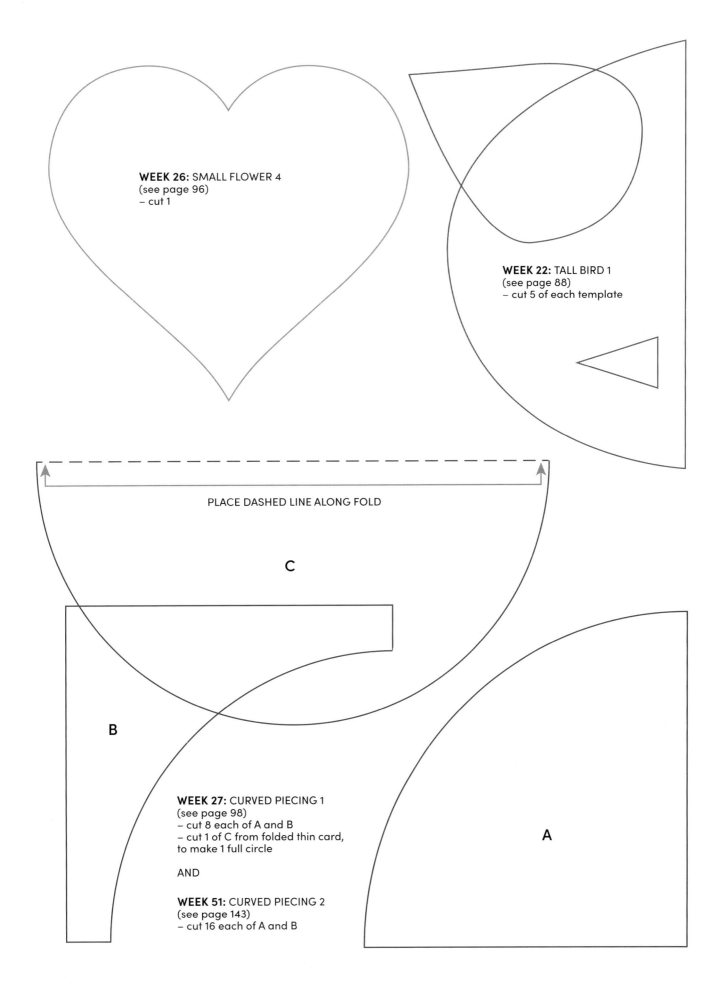

WEEK 26: SMALL FLOWER 4
(see page 96)
– cut 1

WEEK 22: TALL BIRD 1
(see page 88)
– cut 5 of each template

PLACE DASHED LINE ALONG FOLD

C

B

A

WEEK 27: CURVED PIECING 1
(see page 98)
– cut 8 each of A and B
– cut 1 of C from folded thin card,
to make 1 full circle

AND

WEEK 51: CURVED PIECING 2
(see page 143)
– cut 16 each of A and B

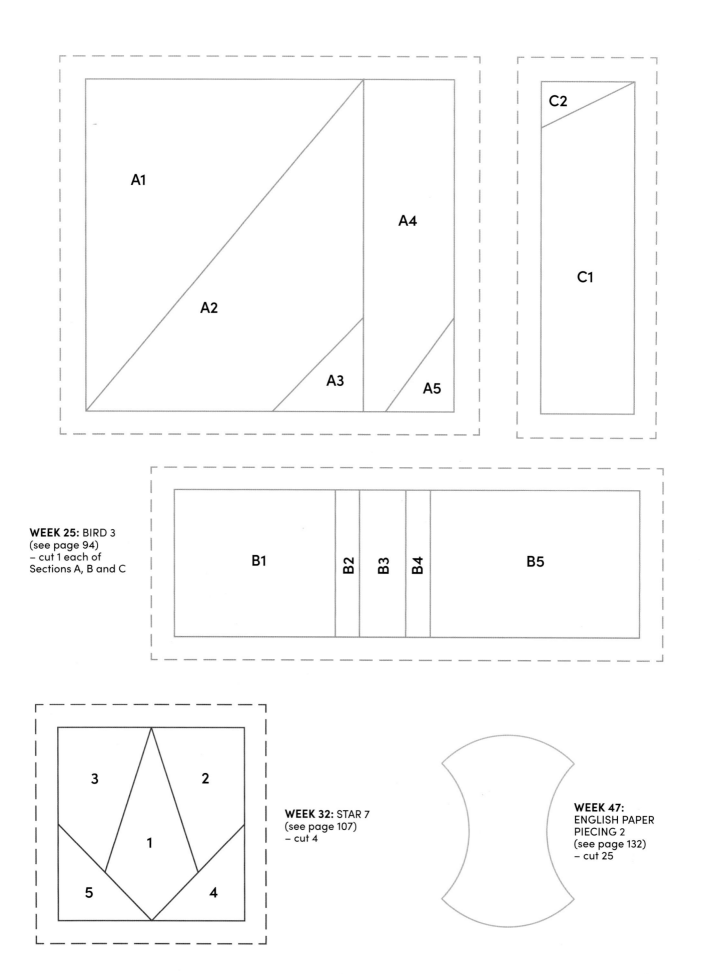

WEEK 25: BIRD 3
(see page 94)
– cut 1 each of
Sections A, B and C

WEEK 32: STAR 7
(see page 107)
– cut 4

WEEK 47:
ENGLISH PAPER
PIECING 2
(see page 132)
– cut 25

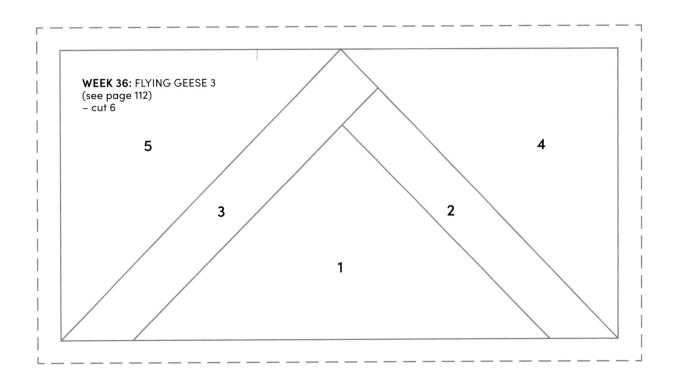

WEEK 36: FLYING GEESE 3
(see page 112)
– cut 6

5

4

3

2

1

WEEK 37: BIRD 4
(see page 113)
– cut 1 of each template

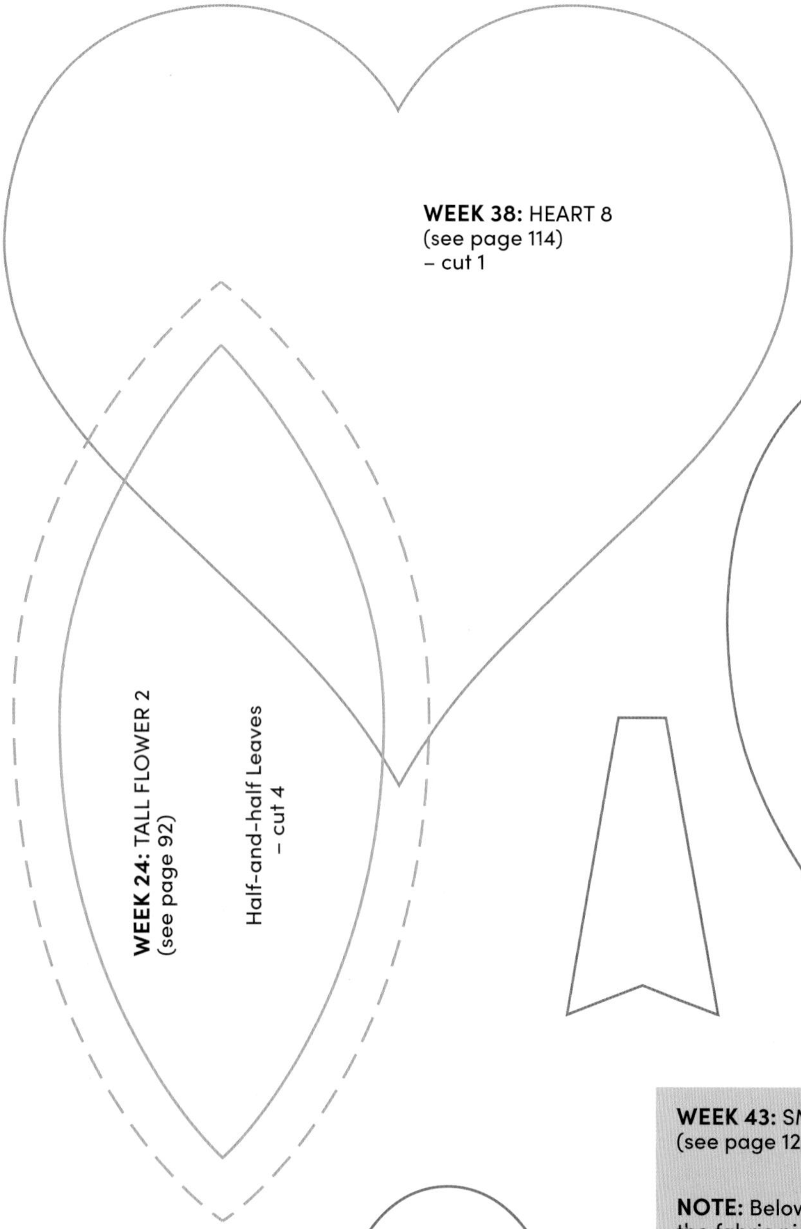

WEEK 38: HEART 8
(see page 114)
– cut 1

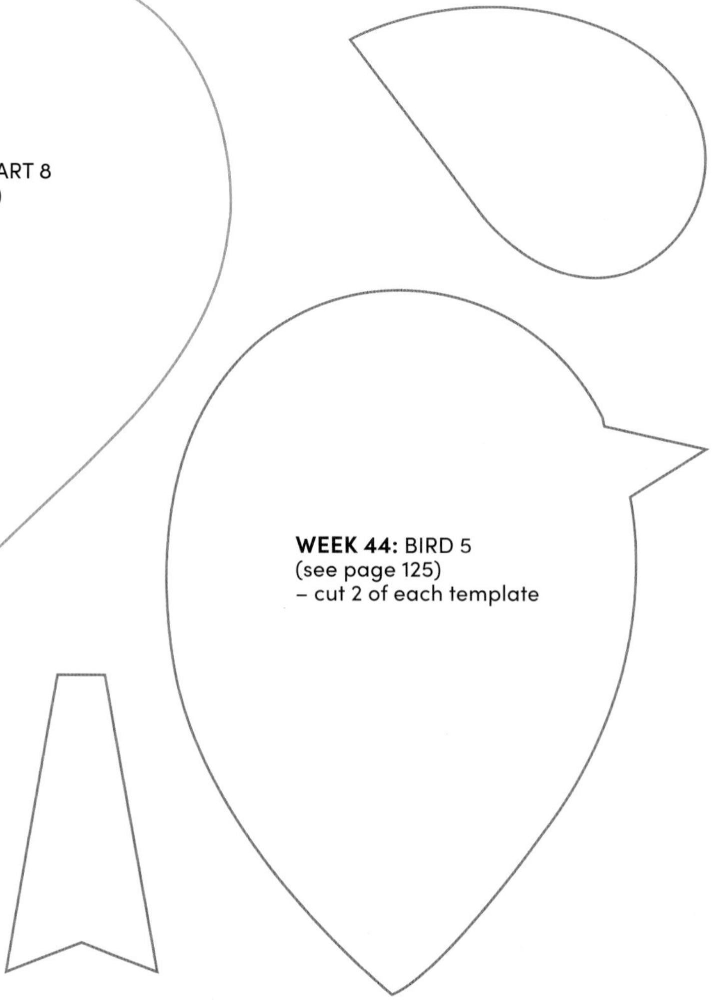

WEEK 44: BIRD 5
(see page 125)
– cut 2 of each template

WEEK 24: TALL FLOWER 2
(see page 92)

Half-and-half Leaves
– cut 4

WEEK 43: SMALL FLOWER 5
(see page 124)

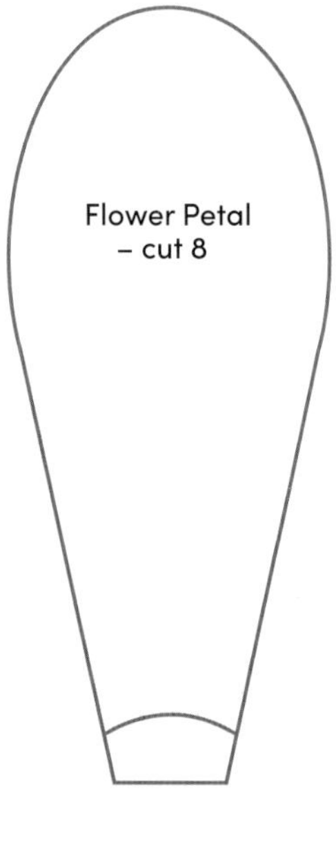

Flower Petal
– cut 8

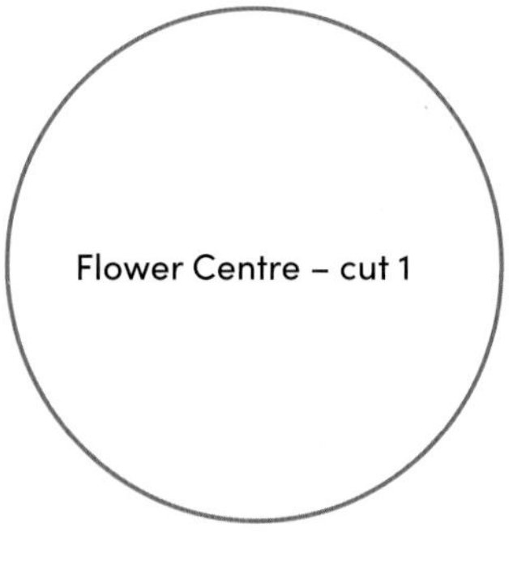

Flower Centre – cut 1

WEEK 43: SMALL FLOWER 5
(see page 124)

NOTE: Below is the placement diagram, showing how the fabric pieces should be positioned on your background fabric. This is not to scale.

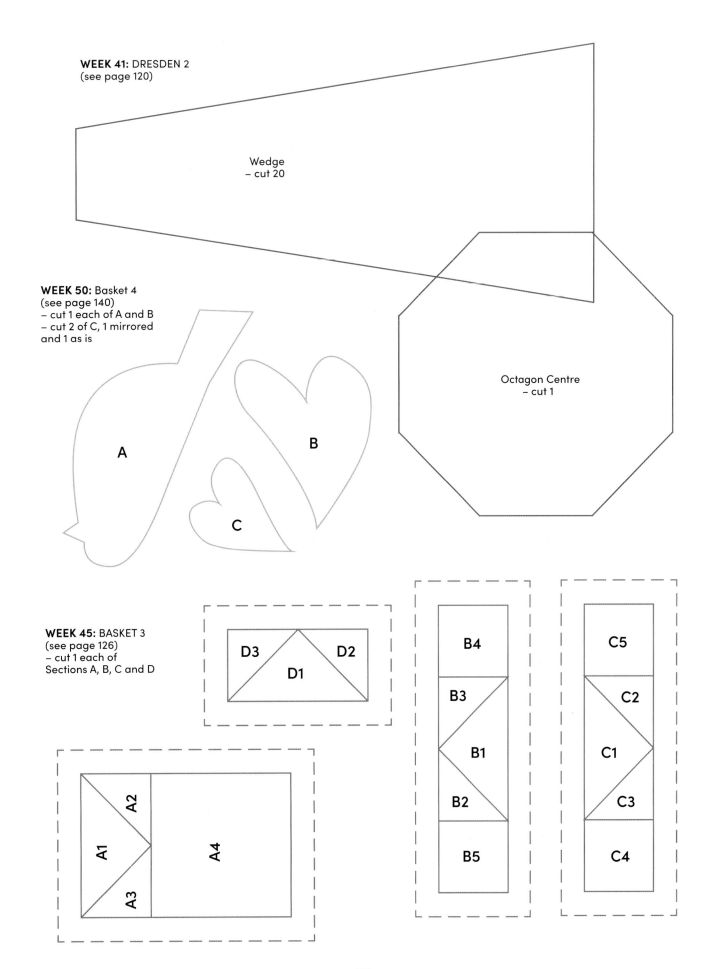

WEEK 41: DRESDEN 2
(see page 120)

Wedge
– cut 20

WEEK 50: Basket 4
(see page 140)
– cut 1 each of A and B
– cut 2 of C, 1 mirrored
and 1 as is

A

B

C

Octagon Centre
– cut 1

WEEK 45: BASKET 3
(see page 126)
– cut 1 each of
Sections A, B, C and D

D3   D2
D1

B4

B3

B1

B2

B5

C5

C2

C1

C3

C4

A2
A1   A4
A3

WEEK 49: CENTRE PANEL 2
(see page 138)

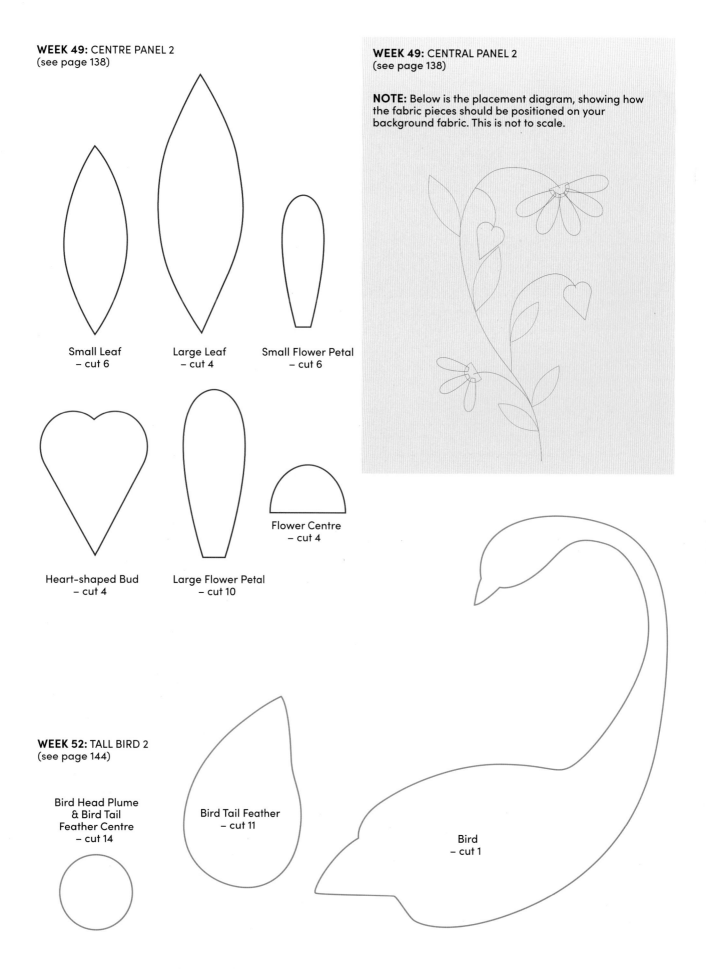

Small Leaf
– cut 6

Large Leaf
– cut 4

Small Flower Petal
– cut 6

Heart-shaped Bud
– cut 4

Large Flower Petal
– cut 10

Flower Centre
– cut 4

WEEK 49: CENTRAL PANEL 2
(see page 138)

NOTE: Below is the placement diagram, showing how the fabric pieces should be positioned on your background fabric. This is not to scale.

WEEK 52: TALL BIRD 2
(see page 144)

Bird Head Plume
& Bird Tail
Feather Centre
– cut 14

Bird Tail Feather
– cut 11

Bird
– cut 1